The Murderer's Son

By Joseph Herr

CHAPTER 1

PEELING BACK THE SCAB

"The trouble with lying and deceiving is that their efficiency depends entirely upon a clear notion of the truth that the liar and deceiver wishes to hide."

Hannah Arendt

Why bring it up now? Why bring up a murder that happened over 45 years ago? A murder that almost everyone has either forgotten or moved on from? Why peel back the scab to this old wound? Me and my sisters have been able to nearly completely wash the pain and shame from this murderous stain away...it has faded to the point that one must look very closely, knowing that it is there to find it. We have each defined who we are and have all built respectable lives despite the obstacles that this stain presented. Why do this now? What was the point of his book? What purpose would it serve? That is what I thought when the call came.

It was a hot late June afternoon; children's laughter filled the air as they played in the backyard sprinkler. I was at my desk doing paperwork and watching them through the window when my phone rang. It was my twin sister Joelle.

"Are you sitting down" she asked. "I just spoke with Dad, he is writing a book about his life and the murder."

"What!? Why would he want to do that" I answered back. "Why bring it up now?" Have you talked to Dorette?

"I don't know" Joelle answered. "He says he's innocent. I haven't talked to Dorette yet."

"We both know better than that" I responded.

"I know. Remember when he told us all that time right after he got out of prison at the Ponderosa, the one on Cedar Street, and he told me again a few years later when Angel and I visited him in Florida way back when.

2

What should we do" Joelle asked. "He says he is approaching publishers and movie producers. He said he has stuff about the Mob and Hoffa...his time in Vietnam...he says publishers are just eating it up."

"We all know he did it. He has told all three of us. Why is it that every geriatric ex-con from Michigan that wants to sell a book has to bring up Hoffa? Did you tell him that you didn't want him to write it" I answered.

"Yes, I asked him not to and told him that I didn't want my name in the book. He said that he would keep You, Me, and Dorette out of it ...but we know people would still know from his name, still remember, and others who don't know about the murder would now figure out who we are. The name Herr isn't a common one in Lansing" Joelle responded.

I then questioned my father's ability to publish his book. "I don't think he can write a book, publish it, and make money...felons are not suppose to be able to profit from their crimes anymore, I think it is the Son of Sam Law."

"What about the woman's children, they must be around fifty or so now...I wonder where they are and what they would think? I wish they could press a wrongful death lawsuit against him!"

"I don't know" Joelle answered.

"Have you talked to his other daughters, what do they think" I asked.

"I don't know" my sister answered.

"He has probably fed them with his lies and exaggerations...they don't know the truth and he tells a

3

good and convincing story...He's a salesman...they naturally want to think the best of their father, you can't blame them for that." I stated.

"No...I think both Jessica and Katherine know." Joelle responded.

"Katherine? That is the other's name?" I asked.

"Yes." She answered.

"They both know that he murdered someone?" I inquired.

"I don't think that they believe he did it." My twin sister responded.

"So he calls you with the anniversary of the murder next week and tells you he is writing a book...what a heartless bastard!" I said.

"I begged him not to do it" said Joelle. "Should we talk to an attorney" she then asked.

"He hasn't done anything yet" I answered back. "Let me see what I can do...I'll let you know. I will call you back later. Talk to Dorette and see what she says."

"Ok...keep me updated" asked Joelle.

"I will. Bye."

I hung up the phone and stared through the window at the purity and joy of children at play. Feeling a sadness come over me, I silently re-lived the pain that this stain had brought me. Viewing the innocence and glee of my daughters and son, I thought back to what my sisters and I had experienced at their age. How different my life was in those tender years. How I didn't ever want my children to know the pain that this wound had brought me. The weight and shame of this cross had already been bared by my sisters and me. I had spent my childhood and young adulthood as "the murderer's son"... I had already paid for my father's crime.

I never had much of a relationship with my Father. Over my forty six years we have probably spent less than six weeks total together, with little other contact or communication. I was twelve when he was paroled. Even after his release, he made little effort to spend time with my sisters and me. My father has never been there for us emotionally or financially, I don't believe he ever paid any real child support, ten dollars a month his last few years in prison, and after he was released and was able to re-establish himself with his career in auto sales, he contributed practically nothing to our upbringing. My mother was afraid to pursue him for additional support; she knew what he was capable of and didn't think it worth the risk of angering him. When my dad did come around he would flaunt his new found success, driving a new Lincoln Town Car and sporting new clothes and expensive jewelry as we subsided on welfare and charity. I have always been fine with not having my father around, although I think that there were times that my sisters have felt differently. I wanted nothing to do with him, I just wanted to be left alone, to live my own life, to be treated and judged for who I was, not for who my father was. Now the specter of this book was looming, and with it potential troubles.

After giving a great deal of thought on how to address this problem, I decided to contact my father's oldest daughter from his new family. Knowing my half sister

Jessica was on-line, she had previously tried to make contact with me through Facebook, and I looked her up and sent her an e-mail. I asked her to try and convince our dad not to publish his autobiography; I gave several reasons why, including how the book may directly affect her and her sister. Hearing no response back, and after regular searches on the internet for a book with no results, I assumed there wasn't going to be a book and didn't give it any further thought until a year later.

The call came from my Aunt Linda, she told me that a cousin in Lansing had just called and told her that a review of my father's book was in the Sunday Lansing State Journal, the date was June 26th, 2011, exactly a year to the day from when Joelle first told me of my father's plan to publish his novel. The review of *Inside Outside* was written by Ray Walsh, the owner of a small independent bookstore in East Lansing. He gave the book positive remarks. I was in disbelief...my father was succeeding, the truth was being disregarded and a new "truth" written.

I searched for the book on the internet and it was available everywhere, Barnes and Nobles, Borders, Amazon, and more. It didn't take long before I decided that I had to order a copy, needing to know what was in it and learn the full contents so that I could determine how I would deal with it.

Sleepless nights and stressful days of anticipation beset the appearance of the paperback. When it finally arrived, I engorged myself in it, quickly scanning the pages in search of familiar stories and tales. I found what I had feared, but there was even more. I was upset and angered as the book was full of half-truths, blatant lies, and manipulated facts.

The book immediately addresses the murder of Betty Reynolds. My dad admitted to being at the scene of the murder that day. He admitted to striking the thirty seven year old mother of two and leaving her at home bleeding from the head and unconscious. He professed his innocence to the murder however, providing a few explanations for who may have stabbed and killed her, as well as a number of different stories to explain why he would plead guilty to such a brutal deed and how he was wronged by the legal system, claiming to have never had his day in court. He accused the late Leo Farhat, his defense attorney, of throwing his case to get retribution at his father-in-law; the two had a long running rivalry. He then leads the reader to believe that there was more than an eight hour time window between when he left Betty Reynolds on the bed to when her body was found, allowing someone else time to commit the murder. He even made the ridiculous claim that his palm print was placed on the knife by detectives. To me there were obvious flaws and questions regarding his story, but to the casual observer I could see how it may be believable.

The most offensive part of my father's book was that it pointed fingers at those closest to me. He accused my deceased grandfather, the man who assumed the role of father to me, and who paid for several attorneys to assist with my father's defense, of being a mobster. He made claims that my mother's father was a made member of the Detroit Mob, connected to the Hazel Park raceway where he never lost when betting on the horses. He claimed that my grandfather controlled illegal gambling in Lansing and made the accusation that he had former Detroit Tiger Denny McClain, as well as former Lions Alex Karras and Dick "Night Train" Lane under his thumb from gambling debts. I guess if you

7

are going to spin a tale, you might as well make it as big as possible!

As if that were not bad enough, in the final chapter of the novel my father had the nerve to state that "One theory bantered about was that Pauline, a jealous wife, followed me out to the Reynolds house and committed the deed." He suggested that my mother may have been responsible for the murder he confessed to and was convicted of; the woman who stood by his side during his trial, and then for another seven years later throughout his appeal. My father included this sentence in his book with absolute malice, aimed at the one person who loyally stood by his side and knowing that my mother didn't, and couldn't have done such a hideous deed. He knew exactly where she was and what she was doing on that day, and she was also questioned by police regarding her whereabouts the day after he was arrested.

I spent the next year going over trial transcripts from the case. I interviewed family members, old friends of my mothers and fathers, as well as a State Police detective who was familiar with the murder and active in the investigation of the crime. I reviewed numerous magazine and newspaper articles on the case. I made a freedom of information act request to the Michigan State Police and was sent the investigative reports as well as the results of Betty Reynolds autopsy. What I found only confirmed what I had already known. Now it was time to finally tell my story and let people know the truth about the murder of Betty Reynolds. My father's book of half-truths, blatant omissions, manipulation of facts, and tall tales had to be corrected. I don't think there is one page that doesn't contain at least one untruth. At times my father's depiction of himself brought images of a dumb luck character who regularly found himself in amazing situations and places as he would brush elbows with various famous and notorious figures of the time.

One thing I know is that people typically believe what they read, especially if it is in any type of published print. Most of the people closely associated with the case were now deceased; there are only a few left who are able to refute my father's new story. I even had a cousin who was around at the time approach me at the Resurrection Church Ox Roast and tell me that she had read the book and thought that the husband, Jack Reynolds, was the murderer. I am certain she thought she was being supportive, but I was incredulous! I immediately filled her in with a few facts that were omitted from my father's tale, and clarified to her who was responsible for the heinous act. For anyone who knew all of the details of that dreaded day there could be no other conclusion; Richard Herr murdered Betty Reynolds on Thursday, July seventh of nineteen sixty six. I wasn't going to let my father's revisionist history be the final chapter, I needed to do something.

My father's book had not only peeled off the scab that covered the wounds associated with his crime, ones that my sisters and I lived and suffered through, he rubbed salt into them. He couldn't possibly think that he was the only one who still had memories of the events surrounding this horrific event. There also had to be information in court files and other public records.

It was left to me to re-tell the truth, if not, it was entirely possible that my father's book would be the final record on the murder of Betty Reynolds, despite the facts. I couldn't let him write the final chapter, full of lies and deceit, and take the chance that one day my children may run upon a copy and accept what was written as truth, that the grandmother they knew may have been a murderer and that their great-grandfather, a man they know I loved, was a mobster.

There is a tide in the affairs of men, and this was high tide. I had no choice, I had to take action, I now had to tell my story, a story that I have so badly wanted to keep buried in the past. My father's crime had cast a shadow of shame on me and my family. We were the unseen victims of his crime, living through the consequences that such a violent act brings. The pain and suffering that we all had once experienced and have never completely recovered from, that we had buried deep into our memories, had now been uncovered once again. The scab had now been pulled back and the wound exposed by my father's fictitious pulp...it was time to set the story straight and mend this wound for good!

Convicted murderer Richard Herr, retired and living in Flagstaff
Arizona where he volunteers as the Toys-4-Tots Santa

The Cover of Richard Herr's book, **Inside Outside: to be continued**

CHAPTER 2

THE MURDER PLEA

"Man is fully responsible for his nature and his choices."

Jean Paul Sartre

Outside the courtroom in a hallway corner of the old county building sat the defendant's wife, my mother, in shock and denial staring off into space, rocking back and forth with my grandmother by her side attempting to comfort her. She was in dismay at what her husband had confessed to her earlier that morning and of what he was about to do in court against her objections. There had been conversations over the previous week about the idea of pleading guilty...defense attorney Leo Farhat was pressuring my father to make the plea...but it made no sense to plead guilty to a crime you didn't commit. My mother had just hired a new attorney, Evan Callanan of Westland, at my dad's request to help with his defense. She had been working hard to assist my dad, pulling extra shifts at her father's club Amedeo's to help with the costly legal expenses.

The new attorney had stopped by the lounge the evening before to retrieve his pay in the way of cash tips that my mother had collected over the previous few weeks. Why had she done all of this if the outcome had already been determined? Why plead guilty? Why give up? My mother truly believed my father was innocent, and refused to hear and believe him when he confessed his crime to her. She was blinded by loyalty to her husband and refused to hear, believe, and accept his admission of guilt.

My mother's mind had to have been searching for answers to the finality of what was about to take place. It was early that morning that the special arraignment had been scheduled. She had left her one year old daughter and three month old twins at the home of her aged Italian grandmother's, she knew at the moment at least the babies were protected from the events which were about to take place, but what now? What would she do? How would she survive? How would she support her children?

Onlookers in the courtroom included among others the defendant's father Richard Sr., his father-in-law Paul "Harry" DeRose, as well as members of the press. The victim's Husband, John "Jack" Reynolds, was not present because authorities were unable to reach him earlier that morning. He learned of the plea later that day after receiving messages from Eaton County authorities.

The murder and trial had gained in notoriety over the prior seven months, with articles appearing in national crime magazines such as Inside Detective and True Detective, regional papers such as the Chicago Sun Times, and state wide in newspapers including the Detroit News and Detroit Free Press, The Holland Evening Sentinel, The Sault Ste. Marie Evening News, The Argus Press out of Owosso, as well as the local paper The Lansing State Journal. It was the type of case where the barbaric nature of the murder coupled with an attractive victim and young defendant would have received national coverage and been discussed nightly on all of the cable news networks had it happened in today's world. Nancy Grace would have had a field day with my dad.

Richard Herr was about to confess to the murder of Betty Reynolds, and tell how it happened.

Before the court of the Honorable Richard Robinson, on Monday, February 20th 1967, in the circuit court room, Eaton County Court House, Charlotte, Michigan

11:25 a.m.

Judge Robinson: It has come to the attention of the Court that there is some question as who is to be the counsel for the Defendant Richard Herr in this matter as the suit proceeds. According to the file, the attorney of record for Mr. Herr presently is Mr. Leo Farhat of Lansing.

It's now come to the attention of the court that Evan Callanan of Garden City, an attorney, has been asked also to represent Mr. Herr.

It's my understanding, Mr. Farhat, that you are acting as Mr. Herr's counsel at the request of his family, his parents.

Leo Farhat: Yes, your honor.

Your honor, Mr. Callanan is here. I don't feel that there is any dispute as between him and me as to his counsel. Mr. Callanan has been requested by members of the family to talk to Mr. Herr as a neutral observer, to review the proceedings here in the court room, and it is with my full consent.

Evan Callanan: Mr. Farhat's statements are a correct statement of the facts, your Honor. I have been requested specifically by the Defendant's wife to come up. I have done so, and I have conferred with Mr. Farhat, and we are certainly in accord.

Judge Robinson: Mr. Callanan, have you had an opportunity to talk with Mr. Herr?

Evan Callanan: Yes, I have.

Judge Robinson: I think now, Mr. Herr, we have gotten to the point where the decision is up to you. The court has no intention and has no right to suggest to you who your counsel is to be. Your family, your parents, your wife, I'm sure are vitally concerned in this matter. But the ultimate decision is yours. And before we can go ahead with this, the Court has to know who is going to represent you.

I don't want to influence you one way or the other. I merely want to know who you wish to represent you, and proceed as your counsel in this matter.

Now, have you had a chance to confer with Mr. Farhat this morning?

Richard Herr: Yes.

Judge Robinson: And have you had an opportunity to confer with Mr. Callanan?

Richard Herr: Yes.

Judge Robinson: Have you reached a decision at this time as to who you want to represent you in these proceedings?

Richard Herr: Yes.

Judge Robinson: Will you tell the court who that is?

Richard Herr: Mr. Leo Farhat.

Judge Robinson: You want Mr. Leo Farhat to represent you?

Richard Herr: Yes.

Judge Robinson: Any further comments by counsel? Mr. Mikesell?

Evan Callanan: May I be excused?

Judge Robinson: You may be excused. Take a recess.

Evan Callanan exited the courtroom and met with my Mother out in the hallway to discuss what had just taken place.

The court resumed a few minutes later at 11:34a.m.

Judge Robinson: Mr. Mikesell?

Prosecutor Mikesell: May it please the court, this is the case of the People of Michigan versus Richard G. Herr. Eaton County Court number three-zero-seven.

Leo Farhat: If the court please, instead of the Prosecuting Attorney reading the amended information which is filed without any objection on our part, we point out that count two has been added to the information, and we asked that Mr. Herr be arraigned on count two, and we wish to advise the court that he has evidenced an intent and desire to plead guilty to count two, which charges him with offense to second degree murder.

With the court's permission, and with the consent of counsel, I believe a brief statement is in order before the court proceeds to discuss this matter with Mr. Herr and take his plea.

Judge Robinson: You want to make a statement at this time?

Leo Farhat: Yes your honor

Judge Robinson: All right.

Leo Farhat: As the court is aware, this matter is scheduled for trial starting Tuesday, February 28th. The case has been pending since last summer. There's been some preliminary motions, skirmishes, some preparations of defense along lines which I will discuss at a later time, and some hearings this morning—a hearing already this morning about Mr. Herr's council.

Suffice to say, your honor, that a great deal of preparation has gone into this case, and much discussion between Counsel and Defense. And Mr. Herr has decided, after listening to our recommendations and reviewing this case against him, and the defenses which we might offer, has decided to enter a plea of Guilty to Second Degree Murder.

I might point out at this time, your honor, that one of the major defenses available to the Defendant was that of insanity. And I have discussed that rather thoroughly with him and given him my impression what I feel his chances to be in an adversary court—adversary proceedings before this court—and he has decided, I believe, to accept the benefit of my advice and counsel.

I have also advised him that he must clearly demonstrate to the court that he is aware of the proceedings and nature of the proceedings, and that he might clearly advise the court of his intentions and his desire to waive the defense of insanity, if the court is to accept his plea.

Now, this morning, we had a hearing to determine who should act for Mr. Herr as his counsel. I should advise

18

the court, however, that prior to that hearing, when I learned that other members of Mr. Herr's family had arranged for Counsel to confer with him—to talk with him—that I immediately gave my consent, although I had no foreknowledge of selection of Counsel. That from approximately nine thirty until a short time ago, Mr. Herr has had the benefit of conference with Mr. Callanan—Mr. Callanan, incidentally, is a classmate of mine in law school whom I have not met since graduation.

I have also conferred with him. I have also advised him it's necessary for him to enter a plea which is acceptable in the eyes of the court.

And the reason I asked for this statement is because it is not every day that we come before the Court advising the Court that a plea to a Murder charge is going to be freely and voluntarily given. It's a difficult decision, not only on our part to recommend, but most difficult for one—for the Defendant to have to accept, and we wish to assure the Court that we have done everything which we possibly can, which we can think of, in preparing for this case and in advising Mr. Herr so that he could make the decision himself.

And I ask the court to arraign Mr. Herr on count two.

Judge Robinson: Mr. Farhat, we never did read the Defendant the amended information as it pertains to count two. Will you read it now Mr. Mikesell?

Prosecutor Mikesell: If it pleases the court, arraignment was had on count one on August 22, 1966, in this case. The Defendant wishes to be arraigned on count two at this time. And I read the amended information in this case, count two, as follows:

Richard G. Herr, late of the City of Lansing, in the County of Ingham and the State of Michigan, heretofore, to-wit: on the 7th day of July, A.D. 1966, at the township of Oneida, in the county of Eaton;

Cont Two: One Richard G. Herr, feloniously, willfully, and with malice aforethought, but without premeditation, did kill and murder one Betty Reynolds; in violation of M.S.A. twenty-eight, point, five-four-nine; contrary to the form of the statute in such case made and provided, and against the peace and dignity of the people of the State of Michigan.

If it pleases the Court, as far as maximum penalty is concerned in relationship to count two, it being a charge of second degree murder, the maximum penalty is imprisonment in State prison for life or any term of years in the discretion of the court trying the same.

Leo Farhat: I might point out to the court, that the practical distinction between first degree murder and second degree murder have also been given to Mr. Herr in the course of our discussions, and the Court might inquire during conference in chambers further in this respect.

Judge Robinson: All right, thank you Mr. Farhat.

Mr. Herr, you have heard the amended charge read charging you with second degree murder. You have heard the maximum punishment which could be imposed on you.

And I notice that there's not a transcript of the preliminary examination in the file, was one held?

Leo Farhat: Yes your honor.

Judge Robinson: Does counsel for the defendant have a copy of that?

Leo Farhat: Yes your honor.

Judge Robinson: Is Counsel willing—the Prosecutor and the Defense Attorney—willing to stipulate to waive the presence of the preliminary examination in the file?

Leo Farhat: I have no objection. I have copies.

Judge Robinson: You have copies? No objection?

Prosecutor Mikesell: I have no objection. I'll see that it's placed in the court file. I do not have my copy with me at the present time, but I will see the original is placed in the Court file.

Judge Robinson: Mr. Herr, you have heard the charge. The purpose of this hearing this morning which we call the arraignment is to let you inform the court as to what your reply to these charges is going to be. You were already here and arraigned on the charges of first degree murder, to which you plead not guilty. Is that correct?

Richard Herr: Yes, sir.

Judge Robinson: Now you have the same options in regard to this charge of second degree murder.

You can plead guilty, in which event the court would assign you to the probation officer for pre-sentence investigation prior to sentencing.

Or you may plead not guilty, or you may stand mute. In the latter event, the court would enter a plea of not guilty for you. And in either event, if you stand mute or plead not guilty, you are entitled to a trial on these charges either before the court without a jury, or before a jury of twelve people selected at random from this county who would sit in these chairs on your right; who would examine the evidence offered against you, the physical evidence; and who, after hearing proofs and examining the evidence, would arrive at a determination as to whether you are guilty or not guilty.

Now, I'm required to inform you that the elements of this offense are as follows:

First, that you unlawfully killed a person, secondly, that you did this with malicious intent; that the intent was entertained preceding and accompanying the act, but that it was done without premeditation.

Now, so you may be better informed what I mean by "malicious intent", I mean that you must have done this act with malice aforethought, the desire or intent to take human life without provocation or necessity.

Now, these are the elements of the offense. The burden is on the Prosecutor to satisfy the court or the Jury that you are guilty of each element of the offense charged, and they must be satisfied that you did so beyond a reasonable doubt.

As you stand here this morning, you are presumed innocent of these charges, and this presumption stays with you throughout the course of these proceedings, including throughout the course of the trial which you may ask for on these charges. Only when the case has been completely tried, and the Jury has listened to all of the proofs, examined the proofs and listened to the testimony, can they arrive at a verdict one way or the other.

If you ask for a trial on these charges, you will be present in Court. You will be privileged to listen to testimony of the witnesses who are brought by the Prosecutor to testify against you. You would be privileged to have them questioned on your behalf by your attorney. You would also be privileged to offer witnesses and proof on your own behalf in defense of these charges.

As I said before—and I repeat—only after hearing all of this information, seeing all of the exhibits and other physical proofs, does the jury retire to arrive at a determination as to whether or not you are guilty or not guilty of these charges.

I mentioned that they must be satisfied beyond a reasonable doubt. Now, by "reasonable doubt", I mean that the Jury must not be guessing or flipping a coin. The scales must not be evenly balanced in favor of the Prosecution and Your favor. The burden is upon the Prosecutor to satisfy the court or the jury beyond a reasonable doubt. This means that the Jury must be satisfied in their own mind to a moral certainty that you committed each element of the offense. Only then can they bring in a verdict of guilty. This verdict must be unanimous. It can not be a verdict of ten jurors or eleven jurors. It must be the verdict of all twelve Jurors.

Having in mind what I have told you regarding the elements of the offense, regarding the procedure which must be followed to establish you are guilty, I ask what your plea is to count two?

Richard Herr: Guilty.

Judge Robinson: Guilty?

Will you come with me, I want to get further (conversation) from you concerning this.

Judge Robinson and the defendant Richard Herr leave the court room and enter the Judge's Chambers for approximately twenty minutes. They then return to the courtroom.

Judge Robinson: Mr. Herr, I pointed out to you the fact that you were entitled to a trial of this cause either before the Court without a Jury, or before a Jury of twelve people, but I neglected to ask you if you wanted a Jury trial on these charges.

Do you want a Jury trial?

Richard Herr: No sir.

Judge Robinson: And your plea is still guilty, as you have given to me before you and I talked?

Richard Herr: Yes, Sir.

Judge Robinson: Your plea of guilty--?

Richard Herr nods his head yes

Judge Robinson: Let the record show that Mr. Herr and I have conferred in chambers, he and I being the only persons present.

And I am going to state on the record as a basis for the Court's reaction to your plea, Mr. Herr, the statement that you gave me as I understood it to be. If in the event I make a mistake, I want you to stop me immediately and correct me. Don't hesitate at this time to interrupt.

Richard Herr: Yes, Sir.

Judge Robinson: You told me this all started when you were the used car manager for Crain's Motors in Lansing. One day Mr. Reynolds approached you to purchase a car. You referred him to your employer, Mr. Taylor, who perfected a sale of an automobile to Mr. Reynolds.

Richard Herr: Yes.

Judge Robinson: There was some difficulty with the title involving a discrepancy in Mr. Reynolds' name.

Richard Herr: Yes

Judge Robinson: That you were told by your employer to get in touch with Mr. Reynolds, which you did on several occasions, and he finally came in to sign the Title correctly. Is this true?

Richard Herr: Yes, Sir.

Judge Robinson: That you then gave the title to Mr. Taylor, your employer, and that it was processed through the office of the Secretary of State. That when it came back therefrom, no lien in favor of the bank was showing. That you were again told to get the title back from Mr. Reynolds—and you inserted at this point that you had met Mrs. Reynolds only once just casually when they came to pick up the automobile. Is this true?

Richard Herr: Yes

Judge Robinson: After being told by your employer to again get in touch with Mr. Reynolds, you again phoned him several times with no success, and so you were finally sent out to the Reynolds' home on July 6th. Is that correct?

Richard Herr: Yes, Sir.

Judge Robinson: You went out there, inquired your way, and finally reached the house. You were met at the door by an elderly lady, and then learned that neither Mr. nor Mrs. Reynolds were home. Is that correct?

Richard Herr: Yes.

Judge Robinson: That you then returned the next day on July 7. That you were met by Mrs. Reynolds. That she rode up from someplace in the yard on a small tractor. That she didn't remember you until you refreshed her memory regarding the car transaction. That she informed you that she didn't know where the title was, and that she went into the house to call her husband to find out where. That you followed her into the house. And at that time she was wearing a swimsuit, two-piece, with a halter. That she used the phone and went in the bedroom. That you used the phone with her permission and you called your three lots back in Lansing to let Mr. Taylor know you were there. Is that correct?

Richard Herr: Yes, Sir.

Judge Robinson: Mrs. Reynolds' two daughters were on the back porch, but they later came in the house.

Mrs. Reynolds came out of the bedroom, this time wearing a pink dress. Is that correct?

Richard Herr: Yes, --just the one daughter.

Judge Robinson: Just the one daughter came in the house?

Richard Herr: Yes, Sir.

Judge Robinson: Mrs. Reynolds came out wearing a pink dress, and went out and told the girls to go to a neighbor's house. Is that correct?

Richard Herr: That's right.

Judge Robinson: That one of the girls objects and Mrs. Reynolds insisted they do as she had told them. And that after an argument the girls did leave the house. Is that correct?

Richard Herr: Yes, Sir.

Judge Robinson: That as the girls were walking out of the house, you walked out to your car behind them and Mrs. Reynolds at that time walked past you saying something you didn't understand, and you then asked her if she had gotten hold of her husband on the phone. Is that correct?

Richard Herr: Yes, Sir.

Judge Robinson: Then she said she had to make another phone call. She went back to the house to do this, and you followed her. After you got in the house, you remained standing in the stairwell of the home. Is that correct?

Richard Herr: Yes, Sir.

Judge Robinson: That she had no success in reaching her husband on the phone, and that you then again asked her if you could use the phone to call Mr. Taylor and let him know where you were.

Richard Herr: I don't know if she had any success on the phone, or not. She did call, but whether she reached anybody, I don't know.

Judge Robinson: She didn't tell you?

Richard Herr: No

Judge Robinson: And you again, with her permission, called your three lots in an effort to reach Mr. Taylor. You got no reply at two of the lots, and talked with one of the salesmen at the third. Is that correct?

Richard Herr: Yes.

Judge Reynolds: Mrs. Reynolds, during this time, was at the sink doing something. That while you were on the phone, it became quiet. That you then put the phone down and turned around and Mrs. Reynolds was standing behind you. That you were hazy as to what happened at this point, but you remember hitting her almost instinctively, hitting her on the head with your fist, then she fell down.

Richard Herr: Yes, Sir.

Judge Robinson: That you picked her up and carried her to the bedroom. That she had something in her hand, you don't know what it was. That as she lay on the bed she looked like she was going to die. And you went to the kitchen and saw a knife on the floor where she had fell. You picked it up, leaning against the sink looking out the window and wondering what to do.

Richard Herr: That's correct.

Judge Robinson: That you went back to the bedroom, taking the knife with you, with the intention of getting rid of her by hiding her body. Is that correct?

Richard Herr: Yes.

Judge Robinson: That you picked her up, carried her outside, down a hill, and down a path, and laid her on the ground. Is that correct?

Richard Herr: Yes.

Judge Robinson: That she at that time opened her eyes and said, "My god, I'm dying."

And you are not sure what prompted you at this time, but you stabbed her with the knife, is that correct?

Richard Herr: Yes.

Judge Robinson: That you left her there, went back to your car, and went back to work. That the car stalled three times while you tried to get it started to leave her on this property?

Richard Herr: Yes, Sir.

Judge Robinson: And your next recollection, you were driving down Waverly Road on your way back to work?

Richard Herr: Yes

Judge Robinson: That you remember washing blood off your hands in the bathroom of the Reynolds' home, but you don't know if this took place before or after you carried her out of the house. Is that correct?

Richard Herr: Yes.

Judge Robinson: Do you have anything to add to this statement?

Richard Herr: No, Sir.

Judge Robinson: Now, Mr. Herr, while we were in Chambers, in the absence of the Prosecuting Attorney or any of his agents, or in the absence of the Sheriff or any of his agents, or in fact anybody else, I asked you if anyone had threatened you with any kind of punishment if you did not plead guilty to this charge. And what was your answer to that?

Richard Herr: No, Sir. No threats have been made.

Judge Robinson: No threats have been made? At the same time I asked you if anyone had made any promises of leniency or favorable treatment to you if you pleaded guilty to this charge. And what was your answer to that?

Richard Herr: No, Sir.

Judge Robinson: No promises made.

Plea of Guilty is accepted. You are remanded to the custody of the Sheriff pending the pre-sentence report.

Mr. Farhat, anything further?

Leo Farhat: Yes, your Honor.

With the court's permission and direction I will ask the Court to request the pre-sentence officer to receive me certain information which I have accumulated during the course of developing the defense which I have proposed to undertake in this case, and that the contents of my information should be forwarded either in digest form or in full form to the Court at the time to be considered by the Court at the time of sentencing.

Judge Robinson: Mr. Vert—our regular probation officer is away at this time, but I'll see that the information gets to him, and he will be directed to contact you concerning this.

Leo Farhat: Thank you very much.

Judge Robinson: Mr. Mikesell, do you have anything more?

Prosecutor Mikesell: I have one other arraignment, if it please the court. It will be rather short.

Leo Farhat: Excuse me. If I might interrupt, I think the court would appreciate having on the record the fact that the Defendant's wife is in the court house but not in the court room, and the Defendant did have an opportunity to confer with her prior to entering his plea. And also in the court room is the Defendant's Father, who has counseled his son, and who has provided the defense that has been offered to him.

Judge Robinson: Mr. Herr, is it true, as Mr. Farhat has stated, that you had an opportunity this morning on previous occasions to confer with your wife concerning this plea?

Richard Herr: Yes, Sir.

Judge Robinson: And you have had an opportunity to confer with your Father concerning it?

Richard Herr: Yes, Sir.

Prosecutor Mikesell: If it pleases the Court, the People will stand with count Two in this case.

Judge Robinson: Let the record show that the remarks of the Prosecutor were with reference to the case of the People against Richard G. Herr.

As the Court accepted the plea, and my father had a moment to reflect on what had just transpired, he had a sudden change of heart. He immediately reached out to Evan Callanan, the attorney he had asked my mother to bring to the courthouse, and fired his defense attorney Leo Farhat on the spot.

Callanan quickly asked the court to set aside the acceptance of the plea. Judge Robinson, not pleased at what was occurring in his courtroom, asked Callanan to file a motion to withdraw the plea, which he did immediately.

The court answered the motion on March 15th of 1967, two weeks prior to the day of sentencing, and just a few days after the defendant's daughter's second birthday. The defendant's motion to withdraw was denied.

Judge Richard Robinson's Courtroom

Eaton County Courthouse

CHAPTER 3

INNOCENT TIMES

"Crime butchers innocence to secure a throne, and innocence struggles with all its might against the attempts of crime."

Maximilien Robespierre

My earliest memories go back to the days at 317 South Holmes on the East side of Lansing. Lansing was a dynamic community, the Capitol City of Michigan, the home of Oldsmobile and the R.E.O. Motor Car companies, and just a mile east of our home was East Lansing, the home of Michigan State University.

The Capitol City had an industrial spirit that was supported by a simple mid-western farmer sensibility. Add in a touch of culture from the University and a dash of sophistication from the State Government and that was Lansing.

We lived in a modest dark blue salt box home with a full covered front porch. This was my first home, the place that my parents held their wedding reception and where my sisters and I celebrated our early childhood, oblivious to the painful moments that must have occurred there only a few years earlier. The times spent in this home were the happiest of my childhood.

My youngest recollections are those of togetherness and unity. I can remember being as young as two, riding in the rusted red radio flyer wagon that my mother would pull three blocks down Holmes Street, then another block east on Michigan to the Schmidt's Market to retrieve groceries. My oldest sister Dorette would walk beside my mother, often complaining because she was not riding in the carriage as me and my twin Joelle rode together to the store and then rotated turns on the trip back securing the groceries in the wagon. I recall what a long journey those four blocks were; sometimes pretending we were on a wagon train in the old west as I was pulled along. I am certain this short trip was even longer for my mother. At times we didn't move more than five feet in a minute's time. We had a car, a turquoise Oldsmobile F85 that my mother had purchased off of My Uncle Ebi, my maternal grandmother's brother, but to save money we often walked to places nearby.

Those were difficult days and we didn't have much. A mother with three young children, attempting to make a good home for them while at the same time assisting her incarcerated husband with support, and assisting with his appeals. My mom made sacrifices at home so that my father would be comfortable in prison. She got very little rest; working long nights at her father's club to pay the bills, then being awaken in the early morning by us kids. My mom wrote to my dad daily, accepted expensive collect calls from him at least once a day, and took the hour trip down highway M127 to visit him in Jackson weekly. She would regularly provide boxes of Romeo y Julieta cigars for him to barter with other prisoners, and she also would bring other items including shoes, underwear, and pricy Sansabelt pants which he insisted on; they represented some degree of status within the penitentiary walls. She did all of this not just initially, but for over the first seven years of his incarceration.

Our home was humble, with a modest front room fashioned with a sofa bed where my mother slept, a coffee table, an ugly green and blue flowered hand-me down chair ripped under the arm with a tuft of dirty gray cotton padding showing, a side table and lamp, and a small 17 inch black and white TV which stood on a rickety wheeled wood and medal stand. A big picture window shaded by the porch and a side window facing the driveway let in a good amount of light.

From the front room you moved to the dining room, which one may have confused for a shrine to my jailed father. Opposite the window which looked out onto the driveway and the neighbor's yellow duplex was a modern styled furniture quality record player that acted as a buffet, adorned with synthetic flowers, statuary, and a framed eight by ten black and white photo of my father. On the walls were displayed several charcoal portraits of our family and others, they included ones of my dad, my sisters and I, my aunt, and in the center, the only sketch that was in full color, a beautiful depiction of my mother. These images were all created by my incarcerated father who had taken up art as he languished in the world's largest maximum security prison in Jackson. He signed every picture DiPaul, for Dick and Pauline. He was a very good artist, and often did portraits of celebrities. Once, Yoko Ono even stopped at the house to pick up a picture of her husband John Lennon; they had been at Jackson Prison protesting the incarceration of John Sinclair who was serving a harsh sentence there for marijuana possession. As for the dining room, I remember it being forbidden for us to play in this room.

From the dining room was a door to the right where there was the small bedroom my sisters and I shared. Most of the room was taken up by a queen sized bed that my twin sister and I were conceived on, and where all three of us slept. In the middle of the bed lay a Bozo the Clown pull string rag doll that happily exclaimed "Howdy, I'm your old pal Bozo!" The room also included a dresser, book shelf, and toy chest. There was no door on the room, instead several strings of wooden beads which stretched to the floor adorned the threshold as if it were some beatnik-hippy enclave from a Jack Kerouac novel.

In the back of the house was the kitchen and a small full bath off to the right, and then in back you would step down into a window enclosed rear porch that doubled as a laundry room which then led out to the back yard or down to the half dirt, half cement "Michigan basement".   My twin Joelle and I would often stand on chairs in front of the kitchen sink, playing in the soapy water and pretending to clean the dishes. We had an old radio in the kitchen and we often tried to sing to the songs we knew. Our favorite was by the Tolkens, *The Lion Sleeps Tonight*, I'm not sure if it was the weededede's or a-wembowet-a- weembowet-a-weembowet that we enjoyed the most!

The second floor of the house had been converted by my parents into a one bedroom apartment to rent out for extra income. Sparrow hospital was only three blocks away and the apartment was regularly rented to nurses.

We were poor but we didn't know it, we were still protected by the naivety and innocence of childhood. For the first few years of our lives we were confined to our house and yard, coupled with visits to the homes of family and an occasional visit to Jackson prison to see my father. There was the nice older woman, Myrtle, who lived in the yellow home next to us that we would say "hi" to when she would come and go.   Other than that, we were rather sheltered. We shared our small dwelling with a black toy poodle named Sassy, and two Siamese cats.

The memories of these times were probably not much different than those of other children, starting the day with Captain Kangaroo, followed by hours of play with my sisters. I liked watching Mighty Mouse and Dick Tracy in the afternoon and playing with my G.I. Joe in front of the television.   I would watch the evening news as Dan Rather reported from Vietnam and would pretend that my G.I. Joe doll was involved in the battles, not yet capable of understanding life and death and the true hardships of war.

My sisters and I were like the three musketeers, constantly at each others side, playing, pretending, and exploring. If it wasn't too cold or raining we were most likely playing in the backyard. As I remember, It was a decent sized yard for a city lot, flanked by our concrete driveway and cement brick garage on one side and a chain link fence on the other that separated Myrtle's tall grass and weed jungle from the trimmed lawn that my mother tended to with her push mower. At the back of the yard was a privacy fence that stood about five feet tall, and behind that fence was a large apartment complex. In the back of the yard was a small metal swing-set, and behind the garage a strip of sand where my Mother grew asparagus, it was the perfect spot for me to play with my toy trucks.

My oldest sister Dorette was always the ring leader, directing the play and making the rules. I was the quiet one, and relied a great deal on my sisters in these early years. We would spend hours chasing each other around the yard, swinging, and playing hide and seek. At times a grass hopper would jump into our yard from Myrtle's for us to try and catch. Or we would try and pull ourselves up to peak over the back fence and look over into the apartment complex behind our home. I was smaller than both of my sisters and was the last to be able to pull myself up and peak into the otherworld beyond the fence. As trivial as it seems now, it was a big deal in our little circle at the time to be able to look over that fence. I suppose it was because the outside world was still a mystery to us.

My maternal grandparents had always played a very active role in my life, and showering the grandchildren with gifts was a regular occurrence. From small plastic swim pools to bikes and once even an electric locomotive complete with tracks that we could ride on.

There is no doubt that Dorette, Joelle and I loved each other very much, I am sure there may have been a small spat here or there, no different than is expected amongst siblings, but we were a team, always there for one another. To us those first few years were idyllic, we knew of nothing better, and we were happy and content. We had each other.

I didn't know of my father's crime at this age, it was never spoken of in front of us, and we didn't think anything strange or unordinary about not living with him and having to visit in Jackson. I was simply too young to understand and that was just how it was. Although we were ignorant of my father's past, it would only be a matter of time before it touched us.

It was a rainy fall afternoon and we had hoped to play outside, but it just wasn't to be. My mother was doing laundry on the back porch and was getting frustrated with us playing and running in the house, passing through the shrine that was the dining room. She sent us to play down in the basement, as we often did, which had a floor that was part cement slab and part sand, with a root cellar built into the foundation. The furnace and water heater sat on a cement island that was surrounded by the mote of sand. I could spend hours down there playing with my trucks, shoveling sand into the dump truck and moving it a few feet, using my back hoe and steam shovel.

On this day Dorette wanted to play treasure hunt. She would burry a ball, the treasure, in the sand and me and Joelle would have to find it, with her telling us if we were "hot" or "cold" the closer or further we got from the treasure. I remember starting to get bored with the game and starting to use my Tonka steam shovel, pretending to search for the treasure when all I really wanted to do was play with my trucks. I was digging deeper than I ever had before when I hit it...maybe a foot below the surface, a hollow box buried within our home. I was so excited; I had just discovered a real treasure chest! Dorette ran upstairs to tell of our discovery, but my mother had no idea what was taking place and dismissed her and the story as playful nonsense. Dorette returned and helped as the three of us pulled at the box and continued to remove sand from around it and tugging until we finally were able to pull the miniature chest out. I remember the box feeling heavy; there must be a lot of gold in it I thought. We opened the latch and there it was, not gold or treasure, but a gun. Our excitement quickly turned to fear.

Dorette took the gun first, and then I asked if I could hold it. It was much heavier than I ever imagined a real gun would be. After a couple of quick seconds Dorette, always the leader, grabbed it back and brought it up to my mother who was just as surprised as we were at our newly discovered treasure.

The gun had belonged to my grandfather; he had reported it stolen years earlier. My grandfather owned a nightclub in downtown Lansing and he had kept it in his car for protection.

There was only one person who could have taken the gun and buried it in our basement. After my parents were married, my father spent some time working nights at the club for my grandfather. The gun came up missing during this period, on a night that my father had been working. My grandfather had left the gun under the front seat of his car, and had left the car unlocked. Why would my dad have taken the gun from my grandfather and buried it in our basement? Was it buried there prior to the murder in Grand Ledge or in the short four day window between the time of the crime and when he was arrested? What did he plan on doing with the gun? These are questions that may never be answered, as is the case for many of my father's behaviors. I do know his actions have touched me and my sisters, and our first small bit of innocence was lost that afternoon in our basement sandbox.

The Herr children in the living room on Holmes Street, 1969

Standing in front of the dining room "Gallery" in 1970

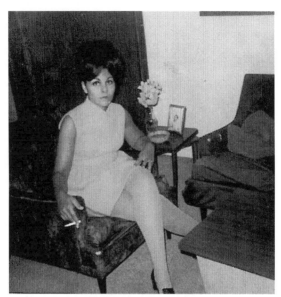
Pauline Herr dressed and ready to go to work
at her Father's club in May of 1969

Picture of Pauline Herr drawn by Richard Herr
while he was serving time in Jackson prison

CHAPTER 4

THE SENTENCE

"Fear follows crime and is its punishment."

Voltaire

Evan Callanan had replaced Leo Farhat as my father's Attorney immediately after the court had accepted my dad's guilty plea. The new attorney immediately filed a motion hoping to withdraw my father's plea, but the motion was denied by the court a few days prior to sentencing.

In the Court's opinion, it was written that "...the decision by the defendant to plead guilty was a considered decision, made after consultation with his wife, his parents, Mr. Farhat, and Mr. Callanan. His conduct and responses at the time were rational and coherent, and he appeared to fully understand what was going on. It is further noted that defendant asked for preliminary examination and such was held on August 3rd and August 8th, 1966, so that defendant in making his plea apparently had some idea of the nature of proofs against which he would have to defend."

The guilty plea was a surprise to many who were expecting a full blown trial. My father's attorneys had regularly asked the court to postpone hearings in order to gather information and plan for the defense. Then there were the many pre-trial hearings regarding evidence and witnesses. Over eight months of planning and preparation went into the case prior to my Father's decision to admit to the murder of Betty Reynolds. My dad's parents had mortgaged their home and contributed over $18,000 to their Son's defense. My mother's father spent an additional $10,000 to provide for extra legal help. This was 1967, when you could buy a pretty decent home in Lansing for significantly less than $20,000. To say the least, the cost in time, energy, and money given to my dad's defense was great.

In an article from The Lansing State Journal following the arraignment and guilty plea, the paper quoted one of my dad's early attorneys to exhibit the public's astonishment to my father's unforeseen decision to admit guilt:

> "Joseph W. Louisell, a Detroit attorney who represented Herr following his arrest, claimed his client had an indestructible alibi. Louisell said Herr was in a doctor's office during the time of the murder and also stated that the doctor would appear in court. Nobody ever found out what happened to the alibi according to authorities."

The truth is no alibi was ever presented in court, most likely because one wouldn't stand up under close scrutiny.

Now the time had come for my father to learn his fate.

The day of sentencing was Thursday, March 30th of 1967 in the Eaton County courtroom of the honorable Richard Robinson:

Judge Robinson: In the matter of the people of the State of Michigan against Richard G. Herr, Defendant, case number three-o-seven.

This matter is before the court for sentencing today. Mr. Mikesell?

Prosecutor Mikesell: May it please the court. The Defendant, on January 20, 1967, pled guilty to a charge of second degree murder in this case, which plea on that date was accepted by this court.

Subsequently, there was a substitution of attorneys and Evan Callanan of Westland was substituted as a Defense attorney for the Defendant and Leo Farhat's services were eliminated.

Following that, a motion was filed requesting that the Defendant be permitted to withdraw his plea of guilty to second degree murder, which was heard by this court.

An opinion on the motion to withdraw plea was signed by this court on March 15, 1967.

Subsequent thereto, there was a motion for entry of an order in keeping with the opinion which was subsequently entered on March 27, 1967 denying the motion to withdraw the plea of guilty.

And, the Defendant appears at this time for sentencing on the charge of second degree murder.

Judge Robinson: Mr. Callanan, will you approach the bench with your client?

Evan Callanan: Yes, your honor.

Mr. Callanan, attorney for the defendant and the Defendant Richard Herr come forward to the Bench facing the Judge.

Judge Robinson: Mr. Herr, do you have any comments to make before the court imposes sentence?

Richard Herr: Yes your Honor.

I don't mean to be disrespectful to this court.--I must be honest for one time. A man's life is at stake, mine.

I've been, I believe, condemned by--press and various newspapers on this--different magazine--black inked-- artists have drawn it up on a million sheets of public print.

And, I've sat over there in this jail for eight and a half months, now, and I haven't been able to say anything on my behalf. True to what the prosecutor said, a few weeks ago, as far as talking to Mr. Callanan, having time to confer with him,--this is true. I had approximately thirty minutes before he came in here to confer with him. And, the previous time when he tried to get into the jail to see me, he was denied admittance.

And, as far as conferring with my wife, in all those eight and a half months I've never had one private moment in all that time to talk to my wife,--by myself.

As far as these reason--I realize Mr. Callanan gave you a set of reasons why I wanted this denied.--One of them would be that Mr. Leo Farhat, my previous attorney-- well, one of the reasons--the main reason is, I was over there, and he sat me on a stool, he was on one side of me, his investigator on the other side of me, and the only thing that was missing was a spotlight,--he was pounding on my legs, "come on, Dick, you know you did it, you know you did it."--"I'm your lawyer; I know what's best for you." And "You might as well admit it, Dick, take the first step." And he just drilled it into me where I had no other choice your Honor.--This was my defense--I didn't know what else to do.

I never once said I was guilty, until maybe a week or a week and a half prior to the time we came into court.--

And, I've spent over there, over eight and a half months in that cell all by myself, no recreation, no

49

entertainment, haven't heard a radio, read a newspaper--The only person I see is a turnkey, three times a day—And, I would have admitted to the Kennedy assassination, if I thought it would get me out of there.

And another reason,--Mr. Farhat--Never once have I ever been shown any details, any report about this case.--

And, the most important reason, your Honor, is I'm innocent of this charge, and I'm not guilt--and I think the public has the right to know what happened out there that day, why did that woman die,--And, I think it's the law of a civilized country to find out why she died.--I didn't do it, your Honor. I didn't do it.--That's all I can say.

Judge Robinson: The purpose of this hearing is to give you the opportunity to make comments of this nature, Mr. Herr.

The Court has examined the pre-sentence investigation report on you, prepared by the probation officer. I'm satisfied from the information contained in that report and from the statement that you gave me, that for your own good and the good of society; you should be removed from contact with society for a substantial period of time.

As much as I hate to do this, it's the sentence of this court that you be sentenced to the State Prison of Michigan for a period of not more than forty years or a period of not less than twenty five years.

Mr. Mikesell, the Prosecutor, will present you with some appeal forms, and I'm obligated to tell you, if you wish to appeal this conviction and sentence, and you do not have funds to employ counsel to do so, it's the duty of this court to appoint counsel to prosecute this appeal for you.

It is further the duty of this court to provide your counsel with such portions of this transcript of these proceedings as are necessary to let him prosecute your appeal.

And, if you wish to take an appeal, you must so indicate to this court in writing within sixty days.

Will you sign the appeal forms at this time?

--Let the record show that the Defendant has signed the appeal form.

Evan Callanan: May it please the court. An appeal has been filed under this date for the Defendant, Richard Herr, copy was filed about two o'clock this afternoon with the court, copy was sent to the Attorney General and a copy delivered, personally, to the prosecuting attorney, Mr. Mikesell.

At this time, I would like the court to set an appeal bond on the Defendant Richard Herr pending the appeal.

Judge Robinson: I prefer that you bring that on by way of motion, Mr. Callanan.

Evan Callanan: All right, your Honor.

Judge Robinson: So I'll have some time to consider it-- If it's all right with you?

Evan Callanan: I'll do that, thank you very much.

Judge Robinson: Mr. Mikesell, any comment?

Prosecutor Mikesell approaches the bench and confers with the Judge off the record.

Judge Robinson: I'm required to give you credit on this sentence Mr. Herr, for the time you spent in county jail.

Do you have that information Mr. Mikesell?

Prosecutor Mikesell: I do not, your Honor, the specific time.

Judge Robinson: Take a seat, Mr. Herr. I should state on the record. Is Mr. Smith here? --Take a recess until the sheriff returns.

Bailiff: Circuit Court will recess.

After a short five minute recess, the hearing resumes.

Bailiff: Circuit court is now in session.

Judge Robinson: To cover a point which I omitted, Mr. Herr, it's the sentence of this court that you be confined in the State Prison for not more than forty years and not less than twenty five years, and credit to be received that in the amount of two hundred, sixty two days, representing the number of days you spent in the Eaton County jail.

CHAPTER 5

WATCHED BY ANGELS

"The golden moments in the stream of life rush past us and we see nothing but sand; the angels come to visit us, and we only know them when they are gone."

George Elliot

I have always felt that despite the stain that has been placed on me by my father's crime I have been blessed to have angels looking out for me; protecting me from the dangers of what can be a cruel and dangerous world. These guardians have taken the forms of family, friends, strangers, and on a few occasions a guiding voice. I like to believe that they have existed as a result of my tainted genealogy, some type of divine balance to the injustice of the murderous brand I entered this world with.

As I had mentioned, we were very sheltered in our early lives and were naive to the dangers that dwell outside of our little world. I was the smallest of the three, and my sisters often acted as my seraphs. My twin Joelle in particular would look out for me, often procuring toys for me, tying my shoes, buttoning my coat, and she would even answer questions on my behalf. Despite the vigilant coddling of me by my sisters, it didn't take long until I encountered the perils that could exist outside our asylum.

As we grew, we were slowly allowed new liberties. We soon were able to play in our garage, long driveway, and even front yard as long as we let our mom know where we were. We were like young chicks slowly straying further and further from the safety of our nest.

It was nineteen seventy, a warm early summer afternoon, and my sisters and I were playing in the front yard when we heard the gargled melody of an ice cream truck in the distance. Dorette darted inside and grabbed some coins from our piggy bank. We could see that the peddler had stopped on the opposite corner of Kalamazoo and Holmes streets, about a hundred yards away, opposite of Crain's Motors. This was a fairly busy intersection, and one that could be dangerous due to the hill that disguised vehicles racing east downward on Kalamazoo Street. We waited in front of our house as the driver of the van full of frozen treats navigated the intersection until he saw his opening and quickly throttled through it. In my excitement I entered the street waiving my nickel to get the drivers attention as my sister's flagged him down from the sidewalk; he never saw me as his attention was most likely drawn to the girls. The ice cream man drove right over the top of me. My sister's immediately ran up the hill to the house and screamed to my mother "Joe is dead". The poor Jamaican driver was terrified that he had just killed a child and wasn't sure what to do. Soon an ambulance came and whisked me down the street to Sparrow Hospital where I arrived unconscious.

The accident left one heck of a welt on my upper right forehead; even today a slight bump is still present. The only thing I remember from this incident is kind of comical and perhaps a little disgusting. It was raining that evening when I was released from the hospital. On the way home my mother, obviously feeling remorse about the incident, was telling me how lucky I was to have been able to ride in an ambulance. When we arrived home we came through the back of the house as Mom struggled to get the umbrella to fold up in the kitchen. She placed me on a chair at the small table in the corner where I was joined by my sisters. I was asked if I wanted some chocolate milk, always a treat that we were not often given. I said "no, my stomach isn't feeling good", but my mother insisted. She picked me up, sat in the seat, and placed me on her lap; she then started to feed me the milk. I tried to drink it, but I couldn't, my stomach was unsettled, I tried to hold it in, but couldn't, I projectile vomited all over the table and floor. It was over a year before I drank chocolate milk again, and have never had much of a taste for it since.

The next spring the city decided to replace all of the sewer lines under Holmes Street. They dug down what must have been twelve or fifteen feet to lay the pipe, leaving giant hills of sand and clay dotting the landscape in front of our home. The construction also forced the rat population out of the sewers and into the neighborhood. After my mom killed a rat the size of a small cat behind our garage, we were no longer allowed to play in the backyard until after the construction was finished. Always looking for a new place to dig with my trucks, and knowing that no cars were able to travel down the street, I made a daily trek down the driveway to play in my new oversized sand box. As the weeks moved on and the work crews started filling in the street, I started to wonder down towards the corner at Prospect Street in search of more sand.

On one such morning, the ground was saturated with water from a strong early morning rain. I had wondered once again down towards the corner where I must have played for well over an hour. After tiring from my frolic I tried to stand and pull myself out of the clay and sand bath but kept slipping back in, over and over again. I would try and take hold of an exposed tree root and pull myself out but I was unable to get a good grip. I began to get scared, not being able to stand without falling and unable to escape this mud bath.

That was when I heard a voice "You stuck in the mud?"

"What" I answered.

"You stuck in the mud" the voice asked again.

I scanned the area to see where the voice was coming from.

"You need some help" asked the voice.

"No" I replied

I then saw a figure move down the steps from the dark porch of the big aged red brick house that marked the corner lot.

"You stuck in the mud" the figure asked.

"No, I'm O.K." I exclaimed out of both fear and frustration.

"No, your stuck in the mud" the man laughed. He was a big and burly man with grey hair and older than my grandfather. He grabbed me by the arm and pulled me out of the street. "There, you're not stuck anymore."

"I wasn't stuck" I exclaimed

"You were stuck in the mud, and you're a stick in the mud" He retorted. "Come up here and let me hose you down. Your mom won't want you in the house like that."

I followed him up the hill towards his house where he pulled a hose from the side and proceeded to spray the mud off me with chilling ice cold water. As I began to shiver, the old man asked "Where do you live?"

"I'm not supposed to talk to strangers, I can't tell you" I replied

"You live in that blue house right there. I know where you live. My name is John, what's yours" he asked.

"I can't tell you" I responded.

"Your stick in the mud" The old man insisted

"I'm not stick in the mud" I insisted.

"You're stick in the mud, that's your name…" John Laughed

"No, my name is Joe"

"No, your name is stick in the mud, that's what I am calling you" John proclaimed as he headed back towards his nesting spot on his porch.

"I'm not Stick in the Mud" I shouted as I ran back to the safety of my home.

A few days later, I got up the gumption and again peddled my red tri-cycle towards the old brick house when John's voice cried out from the dark front porch "Hey, it's Stick in the Mud".

I once again reminded him that my name was Joe, but the old grey hair insisted on my new nickname. He then invited me to join him on his porch where another elderly man sat rocking. His name was Tom.

John was a widowed world war one veteran who lived in the large house on the corner with the other Great War veteran, Tom. The home was sort of a half way house, divided into several apartments for returning veterans to help them get re-integrated back into society. John and Tom were in charge of the house and would spend everyday, rain or shine, sitting and rocking up on the porch, reading the dailys, whittling, feeding the squirrels, and chatting. You may even see them sitting there rocking and chatting in mid winter. They saw everything that happened along that street and had been watching me play for some time. They never called me by my name as long as I knew them; to them I was always greeted as "Stick in the Mud."

I soon became a regular guest on John and Tom's porch, listening to their stories and jokes, watching the neighbors come and go. There were times when they would share a lemonade or ice tea, and on occasion some pretzels, and they showed me how to shuck peanuts which we shared with the many squirrels that lived in the oaks surrounding their home. These were good men, patriotic men who dedicated the remainder of their lives to helping others. They were from another time, a slower time, and a time when neighbors looked out for and helped each other.

With my regular visits to see the friendly old neighbors, my sisters also soon became acquainted with my new pals. It became part of my daily routine to walk down and say hi to the fellows. On one particular day, Dorette and I walked down to visit, but John and Tom were not at their regular perch on the porch. A young man living at the house spotted us and said that he wanted to show us something. I had never seen this man before. He was slight of build with unkempt long hair, a scraggly mustache and beard; he looked similar to those I have seen since of a young Charles Manson.

Dorette and I followed him along the side of the brick house to the side door and stairwell that led down to his room. He opened the old red wooden door which had an American Flag draped across the window to keep any light out. The room was dark with only a flicker of candlelight coming from a corner table and it had the scent of incense wafting in the air. There was a flag with a map of Vietnam draped on the chipped paint cement brick wall which framed a dirty mattress on the floor.

The stranger proudly showed us some of the medals he had won in Southeast Asia, and then pulled out his biggest trophy, a long skinny knife. The knife was a spoil of war, a trophy taken from the enemy. The thin man proceeded to demonstrate to us it's sharpness by cutting off a piece of his long greasy hair. The knife sliced through his locks like butter. The man then suddenly slammed the knife into the wooden table beside his bed and screamed "now leave". Shocked and startled, Dorette grabbed my hand and we started to leave. The man then shouted angrily grabbing Dorette's arm "No, she stays, you get out of here!" He then pushed me out the door.

Not knowing what to do, I immediately ran to the front of the house and pounded on the front door for what seemed like forever but was probably only a handful of seconds. Tom came to the door and asked with hostility "What the heck are you pounding on the door for?" I quickly explained to my older friend what had happened and he immediately raced down to the room and grabbed the stranger. Tom must have been in his late sixties or early seventies, but he threw the young soldier around like a paper doll, as if he were Saint Michael slaying a serpent. He yelled at me and Dorette to get out of there. We ran home and Dorette made me promise not to tell mom or anyone else what happened. I have kept my promise for forty years, this is the first time I have mentioned the incident since.

It had been a few weeks and I hadn't gone down to visit my old friends since the day with the stranger. John and Tom saw me playing out on the sidewalk and they called out to me "Hey stick in the Mud, aren't you going to come over?" I came over and asked about the Stranger, the first fallen angel I can remember meeting, and John assured me that he would not be around anymore.

Over the years Tom and John were always there with a watchful eye from afar, as they recued me from neighborhood bullies on a few occasions. I am certain that they must have witnessed me getting run over by the Good Humor man from their perch. They knew everything that happened along that block, and knowing of their daily routine of reading the papers, I am sure they were also well aware of my father and his crime, but they never gave mention and always treated me and my sisters well. I continued to visit both almost weekly into my high school years until they passed.

Despite all of our new found liberties, whether we were aware of it or not, there were always watchful eyes on us, both good and evil. Years after the crime it wasn't uncommon for a car to drive by our home and someone yell "Murderer". I clearly remember this happening on a few occasions and not understanding or comprehending what was being said as the speech was usually muffled by a quickly departing vehicle. Our home address had been listed in every story about the murder after my father's arrest. The local paper wrote that my father had been arrested at home and gave out the address, when in actuality he was arrested coming out of a doctor's office on Michigan Avenue. Every story in the local paper on the Betty Reynolds murder, or on my father's trial and appeal, continued to mistakenly mention that he was arrested at his home, 317 S.

Holmes. This irresponsible and lazy journalism put an added target on us and our home.

Having a police car parked near our house was a good way of keeping the unwanted drive byes at bay. My mother was an attractive woman, one that most men would notice. Two men in particular who took a liking to her just happened to be in Law enforcement.

One such man was an Ingham County Sheriff's deputy named Eddie. The deputy did some vice work and met my mother at Amedeus, which was Lansing's first topless nightclub. He attempted to court my mother for a few months and I am sure she enjoyed the attention. Eddie didn't seem to like us kids much however, although he made some half hearted attempts to interact with us and even tried to teach Joelle and I how to tie our shoes. I didn't learn to tie my shoes and Eddie failed to win my mother's heart, she remained faithful and dedicated to my father who I don't believe was equally faithful while he was in prison. Eddie eventually gave up perusing my mother, he would later disappear, it was rumored that he went deep undercover investigating narcotics trafficking.

The other officer who took notice of my mother was not nearly as aggressive as Eddie, and the only reason I believe he was interested in my mom was due to his actions. He never made any overt attempts to court her other than a few requests asking us kids to tell her "Hi", but for more than a few years Officer Shaw's Lansing Police Department cruiser was a fixture in front of, or near our house, both on Holmes Street, and then later when we moved down around the corner onto Prospect street. He was a nice man who often opened his patrol car up to us kids and other children in the neighborhood; he would let us sit in the passenger seat as he visited with us. As children, we always looked forward to seeing Officer Shaw. In hindsight, I am certain that the presence of his patrol car near our home kept us safe.

Sometimes we don't immediately recognize the impact others have on our lives, how small and seemingly minor acts can have a meaningful effect on us long after they occur. At other times we can be so caught up in resisting and challenging the effects of others that we are unable to appreciate the kind acts of cherubs. We were lucky enough to have been surrounded by many angels; friends, neighbors, and relatives. We benefited from a close Italian family and extended family that helped keep us safe from outside dangers.
Unfortunately, not all dangers come from the outside.

CHAPTER 6

THE INVESTIGATION

*"Wisdom is not acquired save
as the result of investigation."*

Sara Teasdale

Jill and Penny Reynolds, ages ten and seven, walked to their next door neighbors as their mother had instructed them on that perfect summer afternoon. Their mother wanted to be alone as she spoke with her sharply dressed visitor.

They didn't recognize the visitor, but their mom seemed to know who he was, yet seemed a bit anxious as she walked with them out the door and sent them off. As they arrived to the neighbor's house they were greeted by Jenny Bush, their 14 year old babysitter, and passed on the instructions that their mother wanted her to watch them. Jenny had been visiting with her friend Linda Corey who had come to the Bush home about forty five minutes earlier. Jenny was unsure if Mrs. Reynolds wanted her to watch the Reynolds children at her home or at the Reynolds home, so she went to ask. The fourteen year old babysitter and the girls walked back towards the Reynolds home that sunny Thursday afternoon until they spotted the strangers blue Ford in the driveway and the girls remembered what their mother had told them "don't come back home until the visitor is gone". They told their babysitter that they should go back to her house until the blue car had left. They turned and returned to the Bush home to wait a bit longer. Jill Reynolds however made sure to get a good second look at the visitor's car. She didn't like the stranger and how he was acting towards her mother. It was one in the afternoon.

At about one thirty, noticing that the car was gone, Jill and Penny returned to their home with the baby sitter. The girls entered the quant well kempt home and immediately noticed that things were wrong. There were blood stains on the floor running from the kitchen to the master bedroom. There were also blood spots on the

walls. Jill, the oldest daughter walked towards her
parent's bedroom and let out a scream.   The bed was
covered with blood. Their mother's white house coat
and a piece of her bikini were left torn and bloodied on
the floor. The large bay window in the master bedroom
was smeared with blood and the side window was
broken out from the inside.

The girls ran out of the house, yelling to the neighbor's
for help. Ronald Armstrong was close by working in his
yard when he heard the pleas. He met up with the girls
who described to him what they had found in their
home. He accompanied the Reynolds girls back to the
house where he witnessed for himself what the girls had
described to him.

He immediately made the call to the police.

"What's the address" the operator asked.

"It's the Reynolds home, thirteen thousand block of
Lawson road, 1-3-7-6-2" the man answered. "The
woman is missing and- there is blood all over the
house."

"That's out of the city...but I will call the Sheriff's office
and someone will be right out" the operator responded.

The Eaton County Sheriff's dispatcher made a call to
detective Thomas Keith. "It's about a half mile north of
Grand Ledge" she alerted the officer. "The Sheriff is in
Lansing and as soon as I can reach him I will give him
the location. From what I hear it looks serious!"

Keith arrived just after 2:30 p.m. where he easily
recognized the Reynolds home by the group of neighbors
that had gathered on the front lawn. There were two

police officers out of Grand Ledge already on the scene interviewing them.

One of the village officers approached the detective and updated him on his findings. "All we can gather is that a man drove up to see Mrs. Reynolds, and when the children came home an hour later their mother and the man were gone and there's blood in the house and a broken window, broken from the inside."

The two Grand Ledge officers then walked with Keith into and around the house. "She could have been taken away by the man in the car. But with all that blood she may have also been taken down to the river" the detective theorized.

"Where's the husband" the detective asked.

"He's manager of the Chapel Hill Memorial Gardens cemetery office, in Lansing. We called there, but he is out right now. As soon as he comes in he'll get our message" the younger of the two officers answered.

At this time, Eaton County Sheriff Elwin Smith arrived on the scene. With the patience and care of a seasoned veteran, the Sheriff met with the young girls and slowly had the two Reynolds children describe to him the events of the day. The children told Sheriff Smith that they had never seen the man before. Their Mother was cordial with him when he arrived, and was not afraid of him as she invited him into the house indicating that she may have been familiar with him and was not afraid of him. The girls described the suspect as a younger man, a bit on the heavier side, with brown hair and a darker complexion. He was wearing a yellow check or plaid sports coat and tie, and a white shirt. He also wore sunglasses.

Based on the Reynolds girl's description, Smith figured the suspect to be around thirty years old. Although the girls told the Sheriff that the suspect was tall, he knew that children typically see men as taller than they actually are. "I figure he's anywhere from 5 feet 9 to six feet" he shared with Detective Keith. The car the suspect arrived in was established to be a 1962 Ford "sky blue" two door. "We used other cars for comparison and that is the one they (the Reynolds children) settled on."

"Nobody at the house has any idea who the man might be" Sheriff Smith told Detective Keith. "Check up and down the road...see if the description of the man or car rings a bell anywhere? Then get it on the air and to the police in Grand Ledge and Lansing."

A small piece of paper was found in the back doorway with the word "POLICE" written on it. The paper was from a notepad with the name Parson Chemical Works-Grand Ledge that was found in the kitchen.

At about 3:00 p.m. John Reynolds returned home after receiving an urgent message at work. He was obviously stunned by what he had seen and heard. He had no idea who the strange man may have been, and provided the Sheriff with a picture of his wife to aid in the search. Mr. Reynolds then quickly sought out his children to comfort them.

The investigation at this time was being treated as a kidnapping, but the intuition of the experienced officers told them something different. "This gets more serious by the minute" Detective Keith told the Sheriff. "Doesn't seem reasonable that a man would attack a woman here, and then take her away in his car with him?"

"I'm afraid she's back there, in the woods or the river. We've got men there looking, but that's tangled, rough and rocky terrain. There's a lot we haven't been able to cover" the Sheriff responded to the Detective. "Call the State Police and see if we can get some tracking dogs."

At 9:15p.m. that evening a tracking dog located the limp and brutalized body of Betty Reynolds, rapidly decomposing due to the heat, and swarming with flies and larvae.

A call went out to the Eaton County Coroner, Dr. Charles Black. Under the eerie glow of flashlights the coroner made his preliminary findings, the victim had been dead for several hours, and judging from the amount of blood around the body, she had been fatally stabbed there. The body was then wrapped and taken to Charlotte where the pathologist would start his autopsy of the victim at 2:00 a.m. in the basement of the Burkhead-Cheny funeral home. A group of officers remained at the scene where the body was located along the riverbank, searching for the murder weapon or other clues. Officers also went back and re-interviewed the neighbors and others along Lawson road into the late evening.

The autopsy found that the death was due to "hemorrhage and shock" with the victims throat being cut to the bone with a fairly dull instrument. Dr. Black came to this determination due to the fact that "neither of the common carotid arteries (in the neck) were cut, as were the esophagus and windpipe." The Coroner estimated that the victim lived for about five to fifteen minutes after her throat was cut. Betty Reynolds was stabbed eight times in the chest, each leaving an inch wide wound. One went completely through the heart to the backbone. There was also a stab wound that went through the scull above the left ear, but did not enter the brain. The victim had an irregular wound on one foot as well as several small cuts and glass shards that were imbedded in her feet. There were also indications that the victim was beaten from bruising and broken skin. There was no evidence however that Mrs. Reynolds had inflicted any wounds on her attacker. Her fingernails had been cut short and there was no breakage to indicate that she made contact with the killer.

The police were clearly distressed over what they knew had transpired at the Reynolds home:

• A strange man comes to the home and the Mother invites him in.

• She either knows him or he is some type of salesman, based on his dress they know he was not there to do any type of repairs.

• They also figured the killer didn't just happen upon the house, he knew who lived there.

• The visitor has the Mother send the children away, and then based on the time window fairly immediately attacks her.

• He pulls off her robe and swimsuit

• Based on the amount of blood in the home a struggle occurs there first, and then Mrs. Reynolds jumps through the bedroom window and runs towards the woods.

• The killer chases Mrs. Reynolds, catches and ties her up, and then kills her down by the river.

Early the next morning Sheriff Smith had police artist Robert Brown of the East Lansing Police Department get a description of the suspect from the Reynolds children, as well as from a neighbor and the house keeper who had seen the man a day earlier when he had come to the home looking for the Reynolds. The oldest daughter, Jill Reynolds, gave a particularly detailed description. Detective Brown had the children look through a list of over thirty recently released felons in the area. None of them were the visitor, but the children were able to show the police artist features like a chin on one, a hair line on another, and ears on another that were like the man that had arrived at their home that morning. This allowed detective Brown the ability to draw such a true likeness of the suspect.

Later that same morning, John "Jack" Reynolds arrived at his home on Lawson road to retrieve some clothes and incidentals. While there he had started to clean up a bit. He went to the kitchen to throw something away when he opened the cabinet under the sink to access the wastebasket. This is when the butcher's knife, the murder weapon, was discovered.

There was some confusion based on the description of the killer's car. The day prior to the murder when the man came to the Reynolds home and was greeted by the housekeeper, he was driving a brown compact –type Ford. It didn't have a license plate on the front the woman noted. The Reynolds girls however described the car that drove into their driveway as being blue, a different car than what the maid and a neighbor had seen the day prior.

The sketch of the suspect was completed early that afternoon and circulated to all law enforcement agencies across the state, soon calls started coming in from as far away as Chicago and Sault Saint Marie. Detroit and Lansing Police had been sorting through numerous tips. From the hundreds of calls received that first day, only one name came up multiple times...Richard Herr. The first call said that they thought the picture looked like a salesman at a car lot in Lansing that they had visited a few months back. Then another call came in identifying the same man working at the lot on Kalamazoo Street. The second caller said he thought the man's name was Herr. A third call came in "...an automobile salesman who looked very much like the sketch in the papers-a car lot on East Kalamazoo Street in Lansing-the salesman was Richard Herr." It was the same name that John Reynolds, the victim's husband, had given when he was asked if he could identify the person in the artist's sketch on the afternoon after the murder.

Sheriff Smith did a background check on my dad and found that he had been arrested on a misdemeanor in February of 1966 in Lansing. This was during a period when my parents were separated and my mother had filed for divorce. The Sheriff procured a copy of the mug shot from that arrest and presented it to the Reynolds children. They identified the man in the photo as the man who they last saw with their mother, my father.

After getting three more calls on the same suspect, Richard Herr, the Sheriff dispatched two deputies to check on the car salesman at Crain's Motors in Lansing. They met with one of the lot owners and reported back to the Sheriff that the suspect had worked at this car lot, but had left the job a few weeks earlier. The lot owner also said that the sketch resembled his former employee. Why Gary Taylor didn't tell the police that my father lived just a few doors down on Holmes Street and point them towards the house I can't say, but he did not.

More calls continued to come in. A man said he bought a car from Richard Herr and the car salesman "strongly resembled the sketch of the man being sought for the murder."

Later that Sunday afternoon, a man came to the Sheriff's department and asked to speak with Sheriff Smith. "I think I saw that man, the one in the picture, it was Thursday afternoon, the day the woman was killed." The witness said he was at the doctor's office with his wife at about 3:30 that Thursday afternoon. "My wife was with me, she waited for me and got a good close look at this fellow, she's sure it's him!"

The next morning, Monday July 11th, the Sheriff sent detective Keith and a State Police officer, Detective Thorton, to Lansing to look into the lead at the doctor's office. The waiting room was busy so the officers discretely made their way into the back to speak with the doctor. They discovered that the patient who had visited the doctor that Thursday afternoon between the hours of 3 and 4 p.m. was named Richard G. Herr, the same name kept coming up over and over. He had received treatment for an injured finger. The doctor said he had slammed a car door on his finger. The doctor's record's showed that the suspect worked at Jack Dykstra Ford on Logan Street in Lansing. He had scheduled another appointment to follow up on his finger that same day, Monday July 11th, at 4:30 p.m.

The detectives then went on to discreetly make some additional inquiries on my father. They went back to Crain's where the owner Gary Taylor confirmed what Mr. Reynolds had told them when he identified my father as the suspect in the artist's sketch. That Richard Herr had met with Mr. and Mrs. Reynolds during negotiations for an automobile. Taylor also told the detectives that he had asked for my father's help in straightening out some problems with the sale. This might explain the reason for Herr's visit to the Reynolds home that Thursday if he was indeed the one who went out there the detective thought. "He could have gone out there to straighten out the car deal."

The detectives also learned that Herr was given a brown Ford Falcon by his employer to use on Tuesday, July 5th, his first day at work at Jack Dykstra. He also used that same car on Wednesday, the day the suspected assailant first went out to the Reynolds home, and had asked a gas station attendant for directions, and then later when he was greeted by the Reynolds housekeeper as he arrived at the neatly kept red cottage on that Wednesday. The following day, on Thursday, July 7th, the day of the murder, my father was given a different car to use, a blue Ford. They also learned that my Dad left the lot at about noon that Thursday, and did not return that day.

Detective Keith then presented these new facts to Sheriff Smith who surmised; "That could explain the difference in the cars, if Herr is the man who stopped there. And remember, the witness to the brown compact Ford said it did not have a front license plate. A dealer's car doesn't have a front plate."

That afternoon the detectives, with assistance from the Lansing Police Department and Michigan State Police, arrested my father as he exited the doctor's office after his 4:30 appointment.

Eaton County Sheriff Elwin Smith following up on leads and taking calls during the investigation of the murder of Betty Reynolds, Friday July 8th, 1966

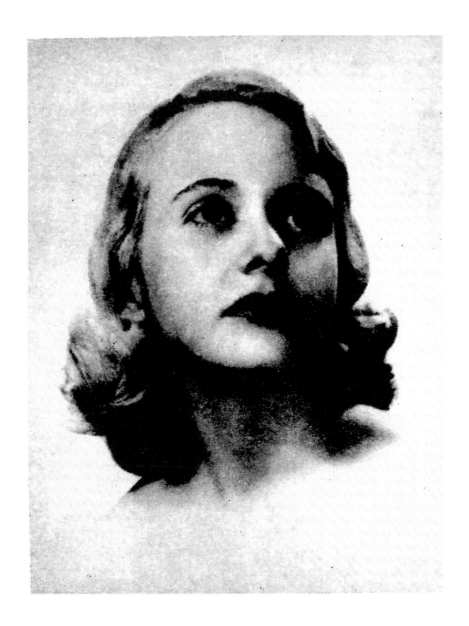

Murder Victim Betty Margaret Reynolds

Officers around the Reynolds home on July 7th, 1966

Police Artist drawing of "The Grand Ledge Slayer" and the
mug shot of then suspect Richard G. Herr

CHAPTER 7

SHIFTING BLAME

"When one person makes an accusation, check to be sure he himself is not the guilty one. Sometimes it is those whose case is weak who make the most clamor."

Piers Anthony

My father, after all of these years, still has not accepted the responsibility of his crime. In his book he has blamed his former attorney Leo Farhat for his choice to plead guilty to murder. He leads the reader of his book to believe the husband, John Reynolds, was responsible for the death of his wife. He also goes on to defame others close to him, including his own mother and father, as well as his father-in-law, Paul "Harry" DeRose. My mother, his strongest supporter and ally during this time, did not escape my father's ire. His statement in his book *Inside-Outside* that "One theory that was bantered about was that Pauline, a jealous wife, followed me out to the Reynolds house and committed the deed" needs to be set straight. I was shocked to read this, and have to believe that my father wrote it knowing it was not true. My mother stood by my father loyally despite the looks, gossip and whispers that were experienced every day when she went out in public. The many nights she cried herself to sleep as a result of her situation are too numerous.

There was an article written by Charles Haas of the Lansing State Journal just prior to my dad's appeal hearing in 1973 that clearly demonstrates my mother's unwavering loyalty. It was titled:

Wife Waits Seven Years-Or Eternity: Prisoners Wife Pins Long Hopes on Hearing

Tuesday, July 12, 1966, seems like yesterday to Mrs. Richard Herr of Lansing, or maybe it's more like a million years since that day she says.

That was the day her husband, then 25, was arrested and arraigned on an open charge of murder in the knife-slaying in Grand Ledge of Mrs. Betty Reynolds five days earlier.

Mrs. Herr says she believed her husband was innocent that day and continues to believe it every day since.

"Almost every single night the facts – the many facts – about the case roll through my head, and I try to put them together. It's all like a giant jigsaw puzzle," She said.

The nude, bound body of Mrs. Reynolds, a 37 year-old mother of two, had been found late in the evening of July 7, about 300 yards from her home. She had been cut and stabbed to death.

With a description provided by Mrs. Reynolds two daughters, an artist's sketch was made, and Herr was picked up after police had received a tip from a caller.

Herr was held on an open charge, and during a preliminary hearing, evidence including a knife identified as the murder weapon with Herr's right palm print on it.

There have been many legal developments and delays since Herr was arrested- legal fees have approached the $20,000 mark, most of them paid by his parents.

Mrs. Herr meanwhile has been trying to provide a normal life for their three children.

"That's the most difficult part – trying to make them understand what has happened to their father.

They know he is in prison – they have visited him often. I don't think they know why he is in prison. They don't talk about it much," she said

Mrs. Herr said that she and her husband have agreed that they can take the pain of separation "because we're older." She says he has put up with the heartaches and strain better than she.

"But it's so hard to be patient – so difficult to keep having any faith in the system of justice," she said. "All we want is a trial. Just a chance to let the people decide after they have heard all the facts. We are willing. Why aren't they? Are they trying to hide something?" she asked.

Herr is scheduled to appear at a hearing Monday at Eaton County Circuit Court on his motion to vacate a guilty plea he made in February, 1967. That would clear the way to the trial the Herrs want so badly.

Mrs. Herr offered a copy of a statement Herr made when he was sentenced to 25 to 40 years by Judge Richard Robinson.

It read in part:

> "I never once said I was guilty, until maybe a week or a week and a half prior to the time we came into court. I've spent eight and a half months in that cell (in the Eaton County Jail) all by myself – no recreation, no entertainment, haven't heard a radio or read a newspaper. The only person I see is a turnkey, three times a day, I would have admitted to the Kennedy assassination if I

would have thought it would get me out of there..."

Herr told the court.

Mrs. Herr says "I had told Dick not to plead guilty, but all that time alone really affected him. He just had to get out of that solitary," she said   He has been in Jackson prison since March 31, 1967.

Mrs. Herr said that she and other members of her family have done quite a bit of investigating over the years- "we couldn't afford to hire someone." She has a thick stack of papers, documents and notes. "We have some very interesting facts-our lawyer Theodore Albert believes he has a good case.

A bid for a trial for Herr was thwarted last summer when Albert was suspended by the Michigan Bar which cited him as a "suitcase lawyer." He is being allowed to practice pending the outcome of his appeal to the bar. "That was just another of the many hurdles we've faced." Mrs. Herr said. "Dick took that in stride. He never quit."

Herr has taken up painting while in prison and had a private showing of his charcoals and pastels in Kalamazoo. He also works as a photographer for the prison newspaper.

Herr also sends flowers to his wife on some holidays and special dates. "He was always very thoughtful that way," she said.

This article exemplifies my mother's unwavering loyalty to her husband. His loyalty has never been reciprocated. My mother's actions the day of the murder, and that whole weekend, have been well documented. As you may imagine, it was a weekend she and others will never forget!

Pleasant, balmy day predicted. That is what it read on the front page of the local morning paper. The temperature was to reach eighty two degrees by noon. July 7th of 1966 had all the makings of a perfect summer day in Mid-Michigan.

My mom woke at seven that morning, my father was already up and getting ready for work, he had an eight o'clock meeting at his new job as a car salesman at Jack Dykstra Ford on the south side of Lansing. He had just started the job two days earlier.

After seeing my dad off, my mom called a few friends, including her close friend Dixie. My mother and her friend spoke of possibly getting together later in the day and maybe doing some shopping. My mother, four months pregnant, then started her job as a homemaker; cleaning house, doing the dishes and watching the baby. She had started to draw a bath for Dorette when she heard a car in the driveway. She looked at the clock and it was ten-thirty exactly. She looked out the upstairs bedroom window and saw it was Dick. He came upstairs and lay on the bed while my mother bathed the baby. My dad shared the happening of his morning, telling my mom about the meeting, how the dealership was to have new sales hours, and how they were presented a new demo package. He had met Mr. Dykstra the day prior and seemed genuinely excited about his new position, this being his third day at his new job.

After finishing the baby's bath, my mom went down stairs to the kitchen where she had started some home-made chicken soup. She continued to monitor the soup, running up and down the stairs as my father played with my sister in the upstairs bedroom. They then ate around 11:30 and afterwards my father went back upstairs to get cleaned up and ready to go back to work. My dad's mom called at that time wanting to know about babysitting in the afternoon, Dick answered the phone upstairs and told my mom it was for her and she took the call downstairs. Dick then left just before noon. My mother was led to believe that he was headed back to the dealership on South Logan, not knowing that he had planned on heading to the Reynolds home in Grand Ledge that afternoon.

In January of 1966, my father had brought Jack Reynolds and his wife Betty onto the lot of Crain Motors as prospective customers. My father worked at Crain's, a small used car lot, for several months prior to his new position at Jack Dykstra. The dealership was just around the corner from his home, two doors down on the corner of Kalamazoo and Holmes. My dad had befriended John "Jack" Reynolds while working at my grandfather's strip club, Amadeo's. Jack was a regular at the bar, he was a skinny small statured meek man who at times could be a bit odd, yet was very likeable. He was a man who enjoyed a drink, liked to talk, and liked to watch the girls dance. He had developed a good report with my father, at times joining him and the dancers to breakfast or to a house party after the club closed. Over time Jack started to share his personal life with my father, including problems he was having with his marriage. It is rumored that both Jack and Betty had been guilty of various infidelities, the relationship was said to be at times physical, with Betty dishing out the abuse, and talk of a possible separation was made on more than one occasion. It was also rumored that Betty once posed for some nude photos while studying art in college. John Reynolds was the manager of the Chapel Hill Memorial Gardens Cemetery, and around the time of the murder it is said that he was often sleeping on a cot in his office rather than going home at night.

It was early January of 1966 when the Reynolds were interested in purchasing a new Oldsmobile 98. My dad must have convinced Jack one evening at the club that he could get a better deal through him than the Oldsmobile dealership. He brought the couple onto the small independent car lot and arranged a meeting with Gary Taylor, the lot owner. The Reynolds ended up purchasing the Olds from Crains, but because of the complexity of the deal my father didn't execute the final sale, it was completed by his boss. Ultimately a discrepancy was noticed; apparently John Reynolds had signed his named differently on the bill of sale, bank contract, and auto registrations. He had used his nickname "Jack" Reynolds on one of the documents, and the bank refused to honor the contract until the names were the same on all the documents. Gary Taylor would regularly walk around the corner and visit my father at home to discuss the Reynolds matter, even when my father was not working. This continued after my dad was fired from the lot, two and a half weeks prior to the murder. Even with my father starting his new job at Jack Dykstra, Gary Taylor came over and discussed the issue of the Reynolds title with him on the fifth of July, after he had completed his first day at his new employer. My dad asked my mother to take the baby out of the house and into the backyard while he spoke with his old boss, so the content of their conversation was unknown to her. She did know however that the talks seemed to upset my father. She told him that he didn't owe the people at Crain's anything, it was their problem, and that he owed them nothing.

Despite the fact that my father had handed over the sale of the car to Mr. Taylor, the fact that my father no longer worked for Crain motors, and the fact that my Dad had to have seen Jack Reynolds several times at his father-in-laws club in the over six months since the sale, he for some unknown reason felt the need to drive out to Grand Ledge and the Reynolds home that day. There had to be another reason?

I suspect that there must have been some type of shenanigans involved with the sale of the Oldsmobile to the Reynolds. That is the only explanation I can figure that explains why my father would feel the need to continue to pursue the issue with the Reynolds title despite having been terminated at Crain's motors by Gary Taylor a few weeks earlier. This is just a theory.

What I know is that Sam Johnson, one of my father's good friends and the Best Man at his wedding, had hired an attorney and was preparing to file a civil law suit against both my dad and Gary Taylor at the time. A little more than a year prior to the murder Sam had co-signed a note at a local bank so that my father could get $1000.00 to purchase a car. Johnson also co-signed the papers on the car deal and his name appeared on the title with my father's as co-owners. My dad eventually went on and sold the car to Gary Taylor and Crain's Motors, and either my father or his boss forged Sam's signature on the title to complete the transaction. Knowing that he had done similar things in the past, it would not surprise me if my father had actually signed the Reynolds papers himself as "Jack" at the time of the sale to skim some money off of the loan, not knowing that Jack was a nickname and that Mr. Reynolds legal name was John. This once again is just a theory, I have no proofs. Only Richard Herr knows his true motive for his visit to the Reynolds home that Thursday in July.

After my father had gone back to work my mom called her mother, my grandmother had wanted to come over and see the upstairs apartment that my parents had remodeled. She had to pick up my mom's younger sister Linda, but would swing by afterward. While on the phone, my grandfather asked my mom about the price of a car, my mom told him that Dick had just left for work and that she would have him call back when he got home.

My grandma and aunt arrived at one that afternoon and my mom showed them the upstairs of the house that she and my dad had converted into an apartment. A new bathroom was installed as well as a small kitchenette. They made small talk commenting on the remodel and played with the baby before the phone rang, it was Dixie calling back asking when My Mom and Dorette were coming over. Hearing the conversation, my grandmother and aunt said goodbye and headed home, they had stayed about twenty-five minutes. My mom then got the baby ready and left for her friend's home at one thirty-five. According to the coroner this was the approximate time of the murder.

My mom drove over to Dixie's where they talked for a while and had a Coke. They then decided to go furniture shopping, they ended up at the Salvation Army store off of Mt. Hope where my mother found a cute white children's tea table with chairs for Dorette. They returned home at just after four that afternoon. Dick came in not long after, around four thirty, and said that he had stopped by at 1:30 to get my mom so that she could help him find the doctor's office. He had smashed his right hand middle finger in the car door at work and they had sent him to see the company doctor, a Dr. Meade on Michigan Ave., but he ended up getting a different doctor. My dad then mentioned that he had also talked to the next door neighbor when he stopped home. This made no sense to my mother because my father had always been very meticulous and precise about time; I am told it was due to his German upbringing, my mother knew she was still at home at 1:30. My father then presented a prescription that he had been written and needed to have filled. Unfortunately they were short on money, and what little cash they did have at the time was spent earlier that day on the child's table.

My father asked my mom to call his mother and tell her about his finger, she came over shortly after and gave five dollars to help cover the prescription. She visited for a short while then left. Meanwhile, my dad spent the rest of the afternoon playing with Dorette and the dog on the living room floor. There was no mention of him going to the Reynolds's home that day. Later my grandmother called and told my mother that my grandfather had heard at the bar that Jack Reynolds wife was missing and it was feared that she had been kidnapped and murdered. It was startling news which came near the anniversary of the murder of my mother's beloved cousin Jerry who had been killed by a knife eight years and a day earlier in Lansing. My mother and grandparents knew first hand of the impact such a crime could have on a family. Jack and his brother Larry were in Amedeo's practically every afternoon and they were well liked. There was genuine remorse for Jack and his family over the tragedy they were experiencing.

88

Later that evening my parents picked up my mother's younger brothers Peter and Greg, and along with the baby drove out to take in a movie at the Crest drive-in theatre in Okemos. The drive-in was owned by cousins of my mother, and my Aunt Rosie who at times worked the ticket window would let them in free of charge. It was a triple feature that night with the main feature being "The Naked Pray" starring Cornel Wilde. It was about a man who was being hunted across Africa by a group of natives. I wonder what must have been going through my father's head, watching that type of movie with the memory of the chase that had occurred in the woods along the Grand River earlier that day so fresh in his mind. Betty Reynolds body was discovered in the woods by the river that evening at about the same time the movie started.

Friday came and went; the local papers were closely covering the murder in Grand Ledge, the first in over thirty years in the small peaceful village. My father went about his day as usual, giving no signs that anything out of the ordinary had occurred. There was still no mention to anyone that he was at the Reynolds home the day before, despite all of the news on the crime. He did ask my mother that morning to take his shoes in to be repaired, which she later handed off to her friend Dixie who had visited and would be driving by the cobbler on her way home. My father stayed out late that Friday evening, but that was not unordinary, despite the fact that He and my mother had been married for less than a year.

On Saturday morning my father left the house around ten and went to get his hair cut at Fred Pirelli's barbershop downtown on Washington square. Afterwards he drove a few miles East on Michigan Ave. and took his watch to be repaired at the Sears Roebuck

& Co. in the Frandor Shopping Center, his father worked there in the appliance department and would eventually retire from that store after thirty three years of service. The timepiece hadn't been working properly, perhaps that was the reason for the discrepancy in time on that Thursday when he said he had stopped home at one thirty?

Meanwhile, my mother and grandmother went to the funeral home to pay their respects in support of Jack and his family. Jack was not at the funeral home at the time, at least that is what was said, but his brother Larry was there to greet them. There were police present at the undertakers, and both my mother and grandmother thought there was one behind a curtain with a camera, most likely to take snap shots and compare them to descriptions that had been given of the suspect they theorized. I personally think that it was Jack Reynolds hiding behind the cover, not wanting to speak to them at that time, having been shown the police artist's sketch and identifying it as my father. My father did not attend the viewing of Betty Reynolds.

Later that evening my grandmother was surprised when Jack Reynolds arrived at Amedeo's. It seemed odd that a man whose wife had been brutally murdered, and who had two young girls who were most likely traumatized by the event, would spend the evening of his dead wives wake at a topless bar. No one seemed to think much of it at the time, because as was mentioned, Jack could be a bit odd. What they did not know was that the day prior, the morning after the murder, Jack had been shown a sketch by the police artist and was asked if he recognized it as anyone he knew? He immediately said that it was Richard Herr. That day a police cruiser made a pass by the home on Holmes Street to see if there was a car that matched the one the victim's daughters gave to the police...there was a light blue Ford Galaxy parked in the drive way. I suspect that Jack and some friends went to the club that evening to search my father out and confront him.

That Sunday morning my parents were wakened by a phone call from my dad's father. He told his son Richard Jr. that his picture was on the front page of The Lansing State Journal. My dad jumped out of bed and ran down the stairs to grab the paper from the front porch. Concerned about his resemblance to the drawing in the paper, my dad suggested that my mother call her father and let him know they were coming over. When they arrived and my dad voiced his concerns about the sketch in the paper, my grandfather asked him one direct and simple question..."Is it you in the picture?" The answer was "No!", and my grandfather then told him "Don't worry about it then." My grandmother didn't think the picture looked like my dad anyhow. My father once again never mentioned that he had been at the Reynolds house that day. They stayed and visited at the home on Lyman Drive for a bit as my grandparents, Aunt, and Uncles played with the baby, the young family then returned home.

Later that evening my father's good friend from his childhood, Mike McCourt, visited my parents with his girlfriend and soon to be wife Pam. Both were officers with the Lansing Police Department. Although good friends, Mike had not visited my dad at his home since my sister's baptism, he was Dorette's godfather. They played cards that night and mention of the resemblance of my Dad to the suspect's picture in the paper came up as well as the bandage on my father's hand. The sketch of the suspected murderer was also being shown now on television during the local noon and evening news casts throughout the state. A few jokes and comments were made and then the discussion turned to something else. What my parents were not aware of was that the artists drawing of the Grand Ledge Slayer had been dispersed to all law enforcement officers in the area two days earlier, so my father's boyhood pal and his girlfriend had to have seen it prior to the Sunday paper and must have been aware that the victim's husband had identified Richard Herr as the person in the drawing. I also have to imagine that they were well aware that the Lansing Police Department were keeping close tabs on my father, perhaps that is what they were doing?

The following morning my dad went to work like normal, he had a follow up doctor's appointment for his finger later that day. My mother did not hear from my father at all that day until she received his call from the Lansing jail late that afternoon, he phoned to tell her he had been arrested coming out of the doctor's office for the murder of Betty Reynolds.

My father called my mother a few times from the Police department, and asked for her to call Fred Abood, a prominent local attorney, for representation. When she called, Abood was with Leo Farhat, who was familiar with my father from a prior divorce filing, and asked his friend for the case based on the fact that he had represented my Father before.

My parent's marriage had not been idyllic by any stretch. They had only dated for six months before getting married and my mother became pregnant a few months prior to the exchanging of their vows. This was not my Father's first engagement, my mom had learned that he had been engaged to a friend of his sister Carols, a Joyce Ritter, but for some unknown reason the wedding was called off. My parents were married at St. Mary's Cathedral in downtown Lansing on August 25th of 1964. Six and a half months later, on March 12th of 1965, their first child Dorette, a baby girl was born.

Richard Herr was a bit of a night owl, and it wasn't uncommon for him to stay out all night doing who knows what? He would occasionally go out on what he called "Commando Raids" in the evening. He would dress in dark clothing and return with various trophies such as the flats of flowers he took one evening from Belen Florist, a bike he may have taken from a garage, and other various spoils. My mother was not happy with this behavior and it made her wonder about stories she had heard of my father peeping in windows as a teenager. I have been told that my father didn't have much of a conscious, and had no feeling of guilt when it came to taking things from others.

My father also had a difficult time holding a job for any length of time. When my parents began dating he was working for Central advertising, pasting signs onto billboards. He then went into sales and got a job at Max Curtis Ford on Michigan Ave., near the Sears where his Father worked. From there he went to work at Crain Motors around the corner from their home on Holmes Street.   His last place of employment was at Jack Dykstra Ford on South Logan, where he worked for just 3 days before he was arrested: Four different jobs in just over two years.

Despite the birth of their first child, my dad behaved as if he were still a swinging single and would regularly go out on the town by himself.   One such incident happened on his first Father's Day; he left before noon not saying where he was going. Meanwhile, my mother prepared a special dinner for him and had laid out some small presents. He didn't come home until the following morning. As you may imagine, such behavior didn't sit well with my mother whose hot Italian temper would greet him upon his return.

My father also seemed to have enjoyed the nature of his father-in-laws business; lipstick and perfume was found on his clothing on more than one occasion, and my mother suspected several affairs. My father was very secretive, and would get violently angry if my mother would open dresser drawers that he considered his. She was not allowed to even open the dresser to put away his laundry. He would position strands of hair in the drawer to know if it had been disturbed or not. I suspect that was because he was hiding his misdeeds in those drawers.

On February 23rd of 1966 my mother filed to divorce my father, she went to Stuart Dunnings, one of the first prominent African American attorneys in Lansing, who was on retainer for my grandfather, to represent her. It was very progressive at that time to hire a black lawyer. Racial tensions in Lansing were high and there were several mini riots and "disturbances" in and around the downtown area during this period. Ironically, a few miles down the road in East Lansing, there was a great deal of civic pride for the Michigan State Football team which included many African American players from the Jim Crow South. The team finished with a Rose Bowl victory in 1965 and went undefeated with 1 tie, the infamous 10-10 game with Notre Dame known as the game of the century, which took place in East Lansing a week prior to my birth.

My father in-turn went and hired Leo Farhat, the former Ingham County Prosecuting attorney who in his prior position had pestered and attempted to prosecute my grandfather and his burlesque style strip clubs with various morality charges, he was never successful. My father had sought Farhat out purposely hoping it would cause some type of additional agitation to my mother.

The divorce came before circuit court Judge Marvin J. Salmon who initially signed an order requiring my father to pay my mother through the Friend of the Court twenty-five dollars a week. As fate would have it, my parents never followed through with the divorce and later reconciled, mainly due to the intervention of my mother's uncle Patsy who was known as a bit of a peace maker; he stressed the importance of family, the difficulty of marriage, and the rewards of it as well.   I was conceived along with my twin sister Joelle the evening of my parent's reconciliation. I wonder what would have happened had they not reconciled. I suspect my mother would have led a much happier life, but I probably would have never been born. I have no doubt however that my father still would have committed his crime. His nature and personality would have ultimately led to this or something similar. The seeds for this murder were sowed in January of 1966.

My mother is not a perfect person, but a murderer she is not! The statement in my father's book that some thought my mother may have been responsible for his butchery could only come from those who knew little or nothing about that day. It is a statement that he placed in his book to confuse and divert the reader from the truth, and to provide a possible explanation, despite the facts. All of the evidence in the murder of the Grand Ledge housewife points to one man, Richard Herr, no one else.

Mr. and Mrs. Richard Herr, in front of Saint Mary's Cathedral in downtown Lansing, August 29, 1964

Mr. and Mrs. Paul A. DeRose
request the honour of your presence
at the marriage of their daughter
Pauline Marietta
to
Mr. Richard G. Herr, Jr.
Saturday, the twenty-ninth of August
Nineteen hundred and sixty-four
at nine o'clock in the morning
St. Mary Cathedral
Lansing, Michigan

Reception
at twelve o'clock
317 South Holmes Street

Wedding invitation for Richard Herr to Pauline DeRose
(note the absence of the groom's parents on the invitation)

The Triple Feature Richard Herr took his family to the night of July 7th, 1966

CHAPTER 8

THE ARREST

"Once men are caught up in an event, they cease to be afraid. Only the unknown frightens men."

Antoine de Saint-Exupery

In the investigation of the murder of Betty Reynolds police received countless tips, but one name kept coming up with regularity, Richard Herr. This, along with my father's resemblance to the police sketch and him being identified by the victim's husband John Reynolds as the person in the sketch the morning following the murder, made my dad the prime suspect. My father was arrested on the 11th of July, 1966 for the murder of Betty Reynolds.

Eaton County Sheriff's deputies and Lansing Police officers arrived at the Ford dealership on Logan Street at 3:20 p.m. There they learned that the suspect had just left to keep his appointment with Dr. Iung. The Ford Fairlane he was driving was spotted and officers followed him to the Doctor's office on Michigan Ave. The Police didn't confront my father at this point, allowing him to keep his appointment with the doctor and receive care for his hand. The Police watched all of the exits, and upon my father leaving the medical building he was immediately met by Detective Tom Keith of the Eaton County Sheriff's department who informed him that he would accompany them to the Lansing Police Department. The detective then Mirandized my father, advising him of his constitutional rights. Detective Keith's police report stated that my father was cooperative and was not hostile, nor did he show any emotion.

Upon arriving at the Lansing Police Department my father was taken up to the fifth floor where he would be questioned. Detective Keith started the questioning, asking the suspect his whereabouts on the afternoon of that July 7th. My father, showing no signs of stress or fear, stated that he had left for work that day at about 7:30. He added that he had been assigned a new vehicle on that particular date. He had been driving a 1966 Ford Falcon, however the transmission was having problems and the Sales Manager, Jim Elder, had given him a 1966 Ford Fairlane to drive on this date. My dad stated that he had been in the salesroom all morning until he left for lunch arriving at his house on Holmes Street at 10:30 a.m. He stayed home until twelve noon when he left to return to Dykstra Ford. He added that it usually takes him twenty minutes to get to work. Before he left the house, he grabbed a can of Spray Nine rug cleaner which he was to take back to Jim Elder to clean the salesroom carpet with. Once in the Ford showroom, my dad spoke with his supervisor and remembered the rug cleaner. He claims he returned to his car at this point which he had locked. He unlocked the left front door and kneeled in the front seat and reached over to the right rear seat and grabbed the rug cleaner in his left hand, placing his right hand on the left door post and slammed the door shut on his finger which was split open and bleeding. He ran cold water on the injured finger but could not stop the bleeding. He stated that Jim Elder helped with first aid, cleaning the wound with hydrogen peroxide and covering it with a flesh colored band aid. Mr. Elder then instructed my dad that he would get the name and address of the company doctor, Dr. Meade, who was located in the medical building on Michigan Ave. (The same building coincidently that my parents family physician, Dr. Haines, had his office.)

My father informed the police that he went to the wrong location and that he could not find a Dr. Meade. My dad then told the detective that he then went home to telephone Jim Elder and get the proper location. When arriving at home to make the call he ran into his neighbor, Jerry Brown, who lived in the yellow duplex next door...he didn't remember what they talked about.

The detective then turned his questioning to John Reynolds and asked my father if he was acquainted with him and his family? My dad answered that he had delivered a new car to the Crain's Motors lot on Kalamazoo Street. The car had been purchased by John Reynolds and at delivery Mrs. Reynolds and the children were with Mr. Reynolds and he was introduced to them. My dad then explained how Gary Taylor, the lot owner, handled the transaction due to the complexities of the vehicle being new. My dad told the detective that he hadn't seen Betty Reynolds since the delivery of the new car. He detailed to them how he had met John Reynolds while working as a bartender at Amedeo's, owned by his father-in-law Harry DeRose, and that Reynolds was a frequent patron. Reynolds would stay until the place closed and occasionally he would take one of the strippers to lunch which is common of patrons to this place. My dad told police that Betty Reynolds had never been with John at Amedeo's.

My father went on to tell the detectives that he had never been to the Reynolds home and did not know where the house was located. He told them that "the last time he had been to Grand Ledge was five to six months ago when his sister got married." He added that she presently lives between Lansing and Grand Ledge and that he has no reason to go into Grand Ledge.

My dad volunteered his finger and palm prints to the Detective, but he would not consent to a polygraph test because "...I had about fifteen months of military police training and have been advised and instructed that the lie detector had proven innocent persons guilty and therefore I have no faith in it and will not submit myself to the machine" he informed the officer.

Detective Keith then asked my father if he was aware of his likeness to the composite picture that had appeared in the Lansing State Journal the day before. He answered that he was aware of it and had expected officers to pick him up for questioning. He added that his father had called early Sunday morning and advised him that he would have to turn himself in, and that he spoke with his father-in-law later that day with a similar line of conversation.

Keith then turned his questioning to my dad's wardrobe, asking about his suits and sports coats. My father responded that he only had two sports coats, the one in the back seat of his car and one at home. The one at home was charcoal black and the other a dark brown. He went on to add that he only had two pairs of shoes, a new pair which he was wearing and another pair that was worn out and that he intended on having repaired.

After the questioning my father asked if he could make a call, and then telephoned my mother at six thirty. He was then taken into a line-up, and then afterwards, made another call to my mother at seven thirty. At seven fifty on the evening of July 11th, my father Richard Herr was placed under arrest for the murder of Betty Reynolds. He showed no emotion and remained calm throughout the entire interrogation and upon his arrest.

In the late morning the following day detectives arrived at the house on Holmes Street where they found my mother hanging up laundry in the backyard. Keeping busy with housework was how she dealt with the stress of the previous day's events. They asked to see my father's sports coats and suits, his dress slacks as well as his shoes and any watches that he had. They asked for the pants that my father had worn the previous

Thursday, and in the pant cuffs they found seeds and fibers from weeds. They also inquired about her whereabouts on the prior Thursday. My mother cooperated fully with the police, let them look around the house, and gave them everything they requested. They presented no search warrant.

The next day, on the 13th of July, police detectives returned to the Ford dealership to try and pin down my father's whereabouts and to check his story. They spoke with the General Manager, Jim Elder, who said he would provide the officers with any information he could.

The Manager stated that on July 7th he returned to the dealership at around 12:05p.m. from his lunch break, returning from the Ingham County Sheriff's offices where he had gone to renew his driver's license. He remembered Richard Herr coming into his office soon after and giving him a can of Spray Nine carpet cleaner to spot clean the showroom carpet. Herr had injured his right hand when retrieving the carpet cleaner from his car and Mr. Elder sent him to see the company doctor on Michigan Ave. The manager remembers Herr leaving at around 12:30. He didn't hear back from my father again until about 3:00p.m. when the new salesman called and said that he was having a problem finding the Doctor's office and didn't have the right location. Elder stated to the detective that he was disturbed by Herr's inability to check the phone book himself and that he had waited so long to call back to the dealership. The manager then added that Herr did not return back to the showroom that day. Elder then turned over to the investigating officer's two pieces of evidence; one was the can of Spray Nine rug cleaner, the other was a rolodex file that contained information on customers that Herr had sold cars to in the past. That Rolodex contained a pink card containing information Herr had made regarding the sale of an automobile to Jack/John Reynolds, the card had been made out on January tenth of 1966. All of the cards were arranged by Month of transaction but this card, which was the very first card with the name John Reynolds, and his address which could be plainly seen. Elder turned the rolodex over to the detectives.

The detective then presented a black and grey checked sport coat to Elder and asked him if it was the one that Herr had worn on July 7th. Elder response was "definitely not".

The detectives had now turned their attention to the automobiles that Herr had used in his short stint at the Ford dealership. The new salesman when hired was first given a 1966 brown/maroon Ford Falcon to drive. The morning of the murder this car was taken back by the dealership because there were problems with the transmission, and my father was given a 1966 Aqua Ford Fairlane to drive. While at the lot, Eaton County Sheriff Elwin Smith noticed a blue 1963 Ford Galaxy that matched exactly the description of the vehicle the Reynolds children had described to police the day of the murder. Records showed that Herr had taken the Galaxy the afternoon of the seventh and had returned the vehicle on the following Monday morning, having kept it over the weekend. The 1963 Ford Galaxy was an extremely fast car, and was the predecessor to the muscle cars of the late sixties and early seventies. Upon inspection, the car showed signs of blood on the headliner. The 63 Ford was handed over to Sheriff Smith by Jack Dykstra and was driven to the State Police Headquarters and turned over to the crime lab.

CHAPTER 9

POOR DECISIONS

"Children begin by loving their parents; after a time they judge them; rarely, if ever, do they forgive them."

Oscar Wilde

For the first several years after my father's arrest my mother remained more than faithful. She was devoted to my dad in ways that seem crazy to me today. She believed my father, or she made herself believe, when he told her that his palm print must have been taken by police while he was sleeping at the county jail and placed on the murder weapon. (This is not the same story my father gives in his book, where he claims detective Keith took multiple prints from him to frame him for the crime.) Her vigilant support, unwavering commitment, and refusal to accept at the time what was so obvious to others seems insane to me. She wrote a letter to my father every day for the first seven years of his incarceration. She also wrote numerous letters on his behalf to the courts and various government agencies pleading to them to grant my dad a new trial. Her dedication to my father, as well as her desperation, is exemplified in the following letter that she penned in June of 1968 to the Eaton County Circuit Court:

> For over two years now we, my Husband, our children, and myself, have been living an indescribable agony. The reason being our belief in our Government. The belief that truth and justice would prevail! We co-operated with the law enforcement agencies and trusted that the truth would free us from this unbelievable nightmare, but instead we were funneled deeper into dilemma!
>
> My Husband gave six years of his life to his country in the U.S.M.C., he was discharged a corporal and has an excellent service record. He fought because he believed in his country and all it stood for. He didn't want his children to be raised in the agony he saw the children in Vietnam endure. If it wasn't so close to my heart I could

find it amusing. But your honor, it's sad to think that a man that risked his life for his country and the truth it stands for can be denied the opportunity to save his life by truth!

My Husband is a good man and an excellent Father, he was a hard worker and a good provider and is very much worth saving. I realize I sound bitter and I am! I was taught as a child about the rights of man in our country but upon adulthood they were disproven by a much wiser teacher and experience.

The truth will be known. My faith in God assures me of that, but what if it is in twenty years, what do I tell my children, that their Father was denied the right of a trial and it was all a mistake and that the people involved are sorry. How do I tell them that they were robbed of a Fathers warmth and guidance because of a big mistake?!

My patience is beginning to fray, but my determination that my husband's beliefs were not wrong and that there is a chance for life are even stronger.

My Husband is innocent, he pleaded for a polygraph test or sodium penethol or both and was denied this also. He was given an electrocardiogram and that provided that he was cooperating and telling the truth but this does no good unless we get into court with the truth and the facts.

My mother's allegiance to her husband was contagious. My grandparents lived next door to State Police Crime Lab Cpl. Donald Bennett, who unknown to my mother and grandparents was actively involved in my dad's case and was one of the first to arrive when Betty Reynolds body was discovered. He was also present at the autopsy. My grandmother would insist to the officer in driveway conversations, not aware of how closely he was associated to the case and his knowledge of the evidence, that my father was innocent. Mr. Bennett would kindly reply "He did it Mrs. DeRose, He did it." Of course Mr. Bennett knew the details of the case and had the proofs. My grandmother, like her daughter, did not want to believe someone so close to them was capable of such a barbaric act. My mother also convinced several friends and family members of my father's innocence, her conviction and passion of her husband's innocence was very persuasive. So much so that even today many still believe he was innocent.

My parents were married for less than two years prior to the murder, and were together as a couple for less than twenty eight months before my father was arraigned for his crime. Despite that short period of time and the turbulent nature of their relationship, my mother gave an additional eight plus years of ardent support and commitment to my dad. This is something that was not reciprocated, as my dad had his share of relationships behind the prison walls. He certainly wasn't celibate.

It was after my father lost his appeal for a new trial that my mother finally succumbed to the forces of loneliness and desperation the life she was living fostered. I don't know if it is right for anyone to judge her, she was under a great deal of stress and longing for adult companionship. Unfortunately, my mother has always made poor choices in men and Tom was no different, my mother was to bring a man into our lives that would change us all.

Thomas Hartford had just gotten out of county jail for some petty crime and was celebrating his new found freedom at one of my grandfather's lounges, The Sir Club. The Sir Club was on what was called the "Sin Strip" of Lansing on Michigan Ave. and was originally a topless bar similar to Amedeo's. My grandfather was having problems with the Lansing City Council renewing his liquor and cabaret licenses. With the city being uncooperative and providing a lot of grief, he figured he would get back at them by turning the lounge into a gay bar. The Sir Club may have been the first outright gay bar in Ingham County. Tom was at the Sir Club celebrating his freedom with some friends one evening when he met my mother. He told her that he was there to "give the fags a hard time." I to this day have never known a heterosexual man who would hang out at a gay bar, but my mother bought his story.

For whatever reason she took a liking to him and they soon started to see each-other regularly. Tom was a tall lanky man, not particularly handsome with a long face and a long nose, a pasty complexion, stringy light brown hair, and awful teeth. He was loud and possessed an obnoxious smart mouthed abrasive personality. He was an alcoholic who often stunk of stale beer, a smell I recognized from occasionally accompanying my grandfather to his lounges some mornings as he collected the prior night's receipts. He also would often reek of another strange smell at times, one I couldn't identify initially, but as time went on I learned it to be that of marijuana.

The first time I saw Tom was when I awoke one night and ventured into the living room, I heard voices on my way to the bathroom and turned to look, he was in the pulled-out sofa-bed with my mother, and he first covered his head and tried to hide within the sheets. I was confused...who was this stranger...why was he in our home at night?

I met Tom a few days later, he was over to "help" us clean out and organize our garage. He pushed us that morning harder than my sisters and I had ever been pushed before when doing chores. I remember how tired I felt holding the make shift card board dust pan as my mother's new friend swept the floor debris toward me, choking and closing my eyes as the clouds of dust irritated them. "What are you, a sissy" Tom asked me.

After organizing the garage, we visited Tom's apartment on Michigan Ave. which was across the street from The Sir Club. The apartment was in disarray with boxes full of clothes, books, and incidentals littering the floor. The walls were adorned with "Keep on Trucking" posters, Bud Man stickers, and other "art" celebrating Zig Zag paper. I knew from visiting the Sir Club with my mother and grandfather that this was not a safe area of town, they had always previously told us not to wander in the area and to stay close.

When we returned home, we went back to work in the garage. I was hoisted up into the banisters with my older sister Dorette as Tom and my mother fed us plywood to create a floor. They then fed us the boxes and crates that contained all of Tom's worldly possessions. This man was more than a friend....he was moving into our lives...and nothing would ever be the same again.

My mother introduced Tom to my grandparents, bringing him to their home for dinner one night. She was no doubt looking for their approval and support for her actions. They were less than accepting however. They knew what Tom was; a convict, a drunkard, a drug addict, and a sexual deviant. Not the type of person they wanted their married daughter seeing, and not the type of person they wanted around their grandchildren.

My mother was hurt by her parent's lack of support, and her way of showing her anger to her mother and father was to keep them away from us children. She went several weeks without talking to them, not allowing them to see us. I remember them coming to the house on Holmes Street and knocking on the door. We were told to go into the basement. My grandparents then went to the back door and knocked. My grandmother still remembers the scared look on little Dorette's face as she peaked up from the dark basement. She waved and called for my sister. My mother, realizing what was happening raced to the back door and screamed with utter rage, telling my grandparents if they didn't leave, she would call the police. Tom hid in a corner laughing like a jackal.

My mother would soon reconcile with her parents, and left the three of us with my grandma and grandpa for a week while she went off somewhere with her new boyfriend. We loved being with our grandparents, so to us it was like a holiday. My mother was still speaking with my father on the phone almost daily up to this point, even after his failed appeal. On this week however he hadn't heard from her in several days, and had started to panic. He called my grandparents to see if everything was O.K., and asked where my mother was. My grandmother told my father that the kids were with them, but that she didn't know where my Mother was, she had gone with a friend for the week or so. My father sensed that something was wrong.

My father's suspicions were confirmed during one of my mother's weekly visits to the Southern Michigan Prison in Jackson. Tom had accompanied her on the trip down M127, she asked him to wait in the car while she visited her husband. About a half hour through the visit, Tom walked into the visitor's room; he had decided to visit a friend who was also incarcerated in the prison. As I have said, Tom was a bit of a smart ass, and with the many friends my father had made behind bars it didn't take long for him to figure out who Tom was. He was furious. He filed to divorce my mother soon after this incident. He also did something that should have had him remain in prison for the entirety of his forty year sentence. He contracted to have both my mother and Tom killed by a fellow inmate who was being paroled. Luck was on my mother's side this time. The contract killer had just completed a hit for another inmate near Detroit, and was on his way to Lansing to take care of my mom and her new companion when he was pulled over by a State Police trooper near Livonia for having a defective tail light. With evidence still in the car from his first killing, the hit man was arrested and ended up serving the rest of his life in Jackson Prison. He had already dug and prepared the holes for my mother and Tom in a wooded area of Haslett, with a bag of lie next to each grave.

Tom would come and go, staying with us for months at a time, then moving out for a few weeks or months after he and my mother would get into a fight. Tom was an abusive alcoholic and my mother fought with him like a hell cat. This went on for many years with the drunkard coming and going from our lives. My mother apparently really cared for this man, and for the life of me to this day I don't know why? He was not a particularly kind person, and was actually quite rude. He was not a good provider and had a hard time keeping a job for any extended amount of time.

112

I suspect my mother found in Tom someone who could relate with her struggles. He was familiar with the prison system and had even spent some time in the Southern Michigan prison in Jackson. He knew how the penal system worked. My mom could talk to him about her frustrations and experiences, and he could relate. He also accepted my mother for who she was. He didn't mind that her husband was in jail for murder. He probably saw it as an opportunity.

The first few months this new figure in our lives kept us busy. He and my mother took us all up to Mackinac Island for a weekend where we hiked the island and visited the historic fort and other sights on the way to and from the tip of the great mitten. We stopped in Indian River to see the cross in the woods, at the time the world's largest. We visited a fire house on our way back home and sat in the large red engines. It was clear that Tom was trying to make a good impression on us kids, but the real demon inside him would eventually show their face.

Tom did not initially spend many days around the house, and would usually arrive after we went to sleep then depart before we awoke. This changed when we moved around the corner to the big yellow house on the corner of Prospect and Rosamond streets.

We arrived at our new big three story home at 1415 Prospect with big hopes and dreams. Instead of sharing a bedroom with no door with my sisters, I would have my own room! My mother had her own room across the hall from me, and Dorette and Joelle would share a room across from the bathroom. We had a large attic we could play in, as well as a finished basement with knotty pine paneling. Off of my room was a very large balcony that sat above our two and a half car garage.

After we moved to the house on Prospect, Tom started spending more and more time at our home. He became a daily fixture for weeks at a time, eventually moving into my mother's room. It was clear that Tom was having a great deal of influence on my mom, and her new circles of friends were not the type of people one should have around young children. My mom at first referred to them as the "Bumskies". They were the type of people who would have comfortably assimilated in Sherwood Anderson's book Winesberg, Ohio, for they were grotesque people. A few of them lived in a strip of houses off of Larch, behind the Bay gas station on Michigan Ave. There was Archie who ran the gas station. There was Ellen and Larry, and a small man who went by "Peanut". And then there was a woman named JoAnne who worked at the Cinema X, an adult theatre and book store on South Logan. My mom would take us with her at times when she would drop JoAnne off at work. Also part of this group was Nancy, who had waited tables at the Sir Club when it was a topless bar, and whose mother was a friend of my father's mother and lived down the street from our home on Prospect. The very last time I saw my Grandma Herr was when she was visiting Nancy's mother Annie-Belle down the street from us.

Drugs and alcohol became common place around us and in our home. Tom would have friends over, playing cards and drinking, swearing and telling crude stories, they would stay late and get drunk. My mom would send us children upstairs. The smell of Marijuana would waft up the steps, we could hear the swearing and laughter from down below intermingled with the music of the Moody Blues and the Who.

These dysfunctional people became a part of our regular lives. Tom would often take us to a place he called 'the

114

drop zone" where he and his friends would do drugs and skydive. It was with Tom that I also made my first visit to Spartan Stadium on the campus of Michigan State University. It was not to see the Spartan's however, but to root for him and his team of "Freaks" as they played against a team of police officers called the "Pigs". I rooted against Tom and for the police that game; I never cared for the "hippie" culture.

A few weeks after we had moved into the house, my sisters and I were playing in the basement where we discovered a false wall; there was a hinge on the knotty pine paneling, and behind this false wall was a plastic bag with hypodermic needles. We were startled and shocked by our discovery. We handed the baggie over to my mother; she said that it must have belonged to the people who had lived in the house before. About a month later we were playing hide and seek in the attic. I started to hide in an overhang opposite the dormer window on the massive third floor when I found another bag of needles. My mother once again blamed the people who had lived in the house before us, but I had hidden in this spot a few times already and I knew the bag wasn't there before. My mother said I was wrong. I am certain the needles belonged to Tom and that she was covering for him. It is also quite possible that it was the very same bag that we had found in the basement previously.

As you might imagine, my sisters and I played a great deal during this period, and having a new home to play in and new places to explore added to the fun. On one particular day we were making too much noise upstairs and my mother yelled up the steps for us to quiet down. We did for a few moments, but before you knew it we were at it again. My mom called us down stairs where she lined us up and scolded us. Tom watched from a chair nearby. She then ordered all of us to take our pants down. My sisters and I all looked at each other, none of us wanted to pull our pants down in front of this man who was still somewhat of a stranger. We were told to do it or it would be worse. We all reluctantly cooperated. We were then to line up in front of Tom where he would whack our bare buttocks with his belt. We all felt abandoned and betrayed by our mother at this time, she was supposed to be our protector, and instead she subjected us to this treatment and this man. To be disciplined in this manner by an outsider was unforgiveable to us, so much so that we all vividly remember these incidents to this day.

Tom seemed to truly enjoy dishing out "discipline" to my sisters and me. He seemed to particularly enjoy abusing me. One evening when I was sleeping he came into my room and grabbed me. I fought him off and screamed. My mother had already gone to bed and was awaken by the commotion. She yelled at Tom and hit him as he left my room. She then yelled at me, what for I don't know. She told me to get my baseball bat and sleep with it under my bed. If Tom came in again I should swing it at him. That was the solution…a baseball bat. Tom left our home that night, but was back not long after. My mother welcomed this man back into our home, even after he came into my room in the middle of the night for an unknown and unexplained reason. This man she had met at a gay bar.

The treatment of me and my sisters while Tom was in our lives was not only abusive, but neglectful. During the winter, if we were too loud or not acting appropriately, a common punishment would be to set us outside, sometimes without our coats or shoes. There

116

would be times when we would be left outside for hours, in freezing temperatures with the wind howling and the snow falling, forced to huddle together next to the dryer vent on the side of the house to catch heat.

As time went on, Tom's verbal and physical abuse towards me continued to increase until one day in the early summer I just ran. I first ran to Tom and John's big brick house at the corner of Holmes and Prospect, but neither of the two old veterans was around. I then ran to our old house at 317 S. Holmes. The door was locked; I tried the door to the upstairs apartment and was able to wiggle it open, so I went up and hid. I curled up in a corner crying, sitting there for an hour or so, starting to slowly nod off, when I heard my mother calling for me. I had been found. I then heard Tom walking up the steps and calling to my mother that the door was opened. My hair stood up on the back of my neck in terror as I tried to figure out how to get away. I worked to open an old window at the back of the house, and was able to slip out onto the back roof above the enclosed back porch just before Tom got to me. He then started to open the window further and stuck his foot out, still in pursuit. I jumped off of the back roof, tumbling on the lawn, and then took off over the wood stockade fence at the back of the yard, cutting through the many different apartment buildings and hiding in the basement of one. When I felt the cost was clear, I took off and ran to my grandparent's house, down Eureka to Michigan Ave., then up Fairview, all the way to Groesbeck. I was eight years old and had just run nearly 5 miles non-stop, fueled by adrenalin and fear. My grandmother was out in the garage when I ran up to the house.

"Joe, what are you doing here" she asked. "How did you get here?"

I told her what had happened.

My grandma then called my mother to let her know where I was and to inquire as to what was going on.

My mother became defensive and irate, and screamed at her mother "You can keep him!"

My grandmother responded "I will! He is a sweet little boy!"

I stayed with my grandparents for a week or so. During the day I would hang out with my Uncle Greg who was eight years older than me. He would have me ride on the handle bars of his bike and ride me to the swamp next to Slater Park. There we would hunt for tadpoles, frogs and turtles. Other days I would watch as he threw cherry bombs into the water, and I would put my hands over my ears as the explosion blew the swamp water and lily pads into the air. My grandfather would come home from his early duties at the bar in the mid afternoon and take a nap on the couch, he always had a cigarette burning in the ashtray and the police scanner blurring on the end table next to him. My Uncle Pete would be in the drive way working on his dune buggy. I would spend hours playing with thousands of miniature toy soldiers that my Uncle Pete had amassed at the bottom of the stairs as my Uncle Greg would play his Beatles "Hey Jude" 45 over and over and over upstairs in his bedroom. We would then eat dinner and fall asleep watching television in the evening. Kojak and Gun Smoke were some of the favorites, as well as Jimmy the Greek on Sundays before the football games.

This was my routine at my grandparents that week until my mother was told that she would lose a portion of her welfare and Aid to Dependent Children checks if she gave me up. She came and picked me up without notice, but this would not be the last time that I went to live with my grandparents.

A few months later, the old grey house on Holmes Street where I had hid and spent my young childhood mysteriously burnt down.

My grandparents were not always around to help my mother with childcare, so she came up with a creative solution to free up four or five hours of time. With Dorette charged with the care of Joelle and me, we would all be given a fifty cent piece and dropped off in front of the old Gladmer Theatre in downtown Lansing. There we would take in a double feature of typically Disney films. Classic movies such as Snow White, Cinderella and Fantasia, as well as new releases like Herbie Rides Again, The Apple Dumpling Gang, and Escape from Witch Mountain; we enjoyed these excursions, but in hindsight, putting a ten year old in charge of two eight year olds in downtown Lansing wasn't the smartest thing my mother has done. Putting that type of responsibility on Dorette's shoulders wasn't fair to her either, and probably forced her to mature quicker than she needed to.

After his divorce from my mother, we didn't hear as much from my father, or visit him as often. During this period my dad had become friends with Ron LeFlore while the future Detroit Tiger star was serving time with him in Jackson Prison. My dad sent me a couple of sets of tickets to see the new ballplayer perform at tiger stadium. Once I went with my Uncle Tom, my father's sister Judy's husband, and once with my Uncle Steve, my mother's sister Linda's husband. I fell in love with the Tigers at that time and fell asleep many nights to

119

the static filled voice of Ernie Harwell on my hand held transistor radio.

My father also bought my sister Dorette a beautiful three piece canopy bedroom set for Christmas during this time from his share of the insurance money from the house on Holmes Street. She had asked him for it during a visit to the prison. I remember being happy for Dorette and the extravagant gift she received, but more than somewhat dissatisfied with my gift that same holiday, a hardbound copy of The Red Badge of Courage.

For several more years Tom would continue to enter and leave our lives. The end of Tom and my mother's relationship came from a fight that was no different than was usual between the two of them. He came home drunk one night and they got into a fight. She kicked him out of the house amidst cursing and breaking furniture. What made this different however was what happened on the following day. Tom and a friend decided to rob the Michigan National Bank branch on South Washington in Lansing. They were caught in the act and Tom was sentenced to a few years in Federal Prison. It was a good thing for Tom he was sent to Federal Prison, I am certain that if he had been sent to the State prison in Jackson he would have had a most unfortunate slip and fall from the fifth story catwalk onto the terrazzo floor below.

When Tom was eventually released after serving his time, he once again showed up on our front porch. I can't remember if it was me or one of my sisters who answered the door, but we were all there in the living room at the time. Tom was made to wait on the front porch while we went and told my mother that he was there. We all emphatically told her that we didn't want this man in our home or around us anymore.

My mother then greeted Tom at the door and spoke with him. We were a bit surprised that she didn't let him in the house. To our astonishment, she told him that he was no longer welcomed in our home and to not come back. We were all shocked, but thrilled. Even though we had voiced our opinions, I think we all believed that Tom was back. Up to that point my mother had rarely put our interests before those of this grotesque man. But now she had found the strength to do what was best for her family, as well as herself.

My mother's poor decisions had always been based on the same error; putting the needs of the man in her life ahead of those of herself and her children. She continually repeated the same mistake, whether it was buying expensive boxes of cigars for my father while struggling to pay the gas and electric bills to keep us warm, or giving shelter to the beatnik Tom at the expense of her children's wellbeing.

I have spoken many times with my mother about my father and Tom and the choices she made during my youth. She acknowledges her mistakes and regrets them. They were poor choices and poor decisions made during difficult times.

They were hard lessons for us all. I have forgiven her for her choices and the treatment I endured during this period, but will never forget. They have shaped me.

Tom Hartford (holding parachute) with Larry Galimore (far left),
and other "Bumskies" at the "Drop Zone"

Program from the Pigs and Freaks football game
that Tom Hartford participated in, 1975

CHAPTER 10

THE ARRAIGNMENT

"Facts are stubborn things; and whatever may be our wishes, our inclinations, or the dictates of our passions, they cannot alter the state of facts and evidence"

John Adams

On August 3rd of 1966 Richard Herr was brought in front of Municipal Court Judge Robert Ballard for his preliminary examination on the charge of first degree murder. The hot and stuffy court room was jam packed; every corner was filled with onlookers, mostly women. One local arrived still wearing the work boots she used while doing her morning duties on the family farm. "It is the biggest thing to happen in this town in over twenty years and I don't want to miss a moment of it." She told a reporter. That same day, famed and controversial comedian Lenny Bruce had been found dead in his hotel room, but the Herr-Reynolds Murder Trial was still the top story in Mid-Michigan.

A large contingent of customers and employees from Amedeo's Night Club made the trip from Lansing, arriving early that morning in Charlotte and gathering for breakfast before the trial in a show of support for my father. My grandmother offered to pay the bill for everyone at the local diner that morning, but was short on cash, not expecting such a large number of onlookers. She ended up having to borrow some money from one of her loyal and long-time employees who went by the name of Brooklyn.

Leo Farhat acted as the lead defense counsel. His services were being paid for by my father's parents, and assisting him was Joe Louisell, a renowned defense attorney from Detroit who was retained by my grandfather to help with my dad's defense.

My grandfather had a confrontational history with Farhat and didn't trust that the Defense attorney would do what was best for his son-in-law. This was despite the fact that Leo was a good friend of his older brothers and was recently a pallbearer at my Uncle Albert's funeral when he passed a year earlier. His niece Patty Farhat was also one of my mother's best friends. Joe Louisell was hired to make sure that my father's Defense was handled properly. Farhat could not have been happy with the addition of the out of town counsel who had made his name representing professional athletes as well as members of organized crime Mafia families. Louisell garnered a national reputation while representing Detroit Lion Alex Karras in his lawsuit against Pete Roselle and the NFL in 1964 when Karras was suspended for betting on NFL games.

Nine years earlier Farhat was the Ingham County Prosecutor and was handling the murder of my grandfather's beloved nephew. At that time my mother's father hired another Detroit attorney, Louis Colombo Jr., to help oversee the prosecution and to make sure that Farhat didn't make a mistake or offer a plea to the perpetrator. Farhat eventually did end up offering a plea in that case and I am certain this weighed heavy in my grandfather's decision to seek alternate counsel in my father's case. My grandfather probably would have hired attorneys to help in both cases no matter what, but the fact that Farhat and my grandfather had a very public rivalry when Farhat was Prosecutor, this type of meddling couldn't have set well with the Syrian barrister. He was a proud man with a big reputation. Today, a yearly award bearing his name is given to an outstanding Lansing area attorney by the Ingham County Bar association.

It was clear from the beginning that Farhat was working for my father's parents, not once meeting with my mother to discuss the case and the strategy for her husband's defense. Instead of a unified effort on my father's behalf, there were two camps. Louisell would help keep my mother informed through the first few sessions.

From the start of their marriage my father's parents, particularly his mother, never seemed to bond with my mom. My grandma Herr was a bit of a socialite, and the nature of my grandfather's businesses coupled with the rather short engagement and marriage to my mother, and then adding in the pregnancy before-hand most certainly embarrassed my paternal grandmother and made her feel uncomfortable about the relationship. Then when you consider my mother's filing for divorce the February before, and the fact that they knew more about my father's past than anyone, and it becomes more understanding. Even as a kid growing up, when they were still living in Okemos it was very rare for us to see my father's parents.

As the hearing began, there was some immediate contention as the Defense was granted access to the police reports over the objections of the Prosecution. The first witness called by Prosecutor Willard Mikesell on that initial day was Detective Thomas Keith of the Eaton County Sheriff's department. Keith was the first Sheriff's officer on the scene, arriving at the small red cottage in Grand Ledge at about 2:45 the day of July seventh. He first testified about the butcher knife that had the prints of the defendant on the blood stained handle described as the murder weapon. Keith said that the knife was discovered "...in a red paper basket "under the sink by the husband, John Reynolds, the day after the murder. He added that "eight or nine people were in the kitchen at the time" Reynolds found the knife. Keith then went on to testify about first arriving onto the scene of what was initially thought to be a kidnapping and noticing blood in most of the rooms upstairs and in the basement, and noting that a window

126

in the master bedroom had been broken out from the inside.

The next couple of witnesses to appear on behalf of the prosecution were Michigan State Police officers. Many of these officers felt a touch of sorrow and conflict at what they had to present. They had gotten to know Richard Herr Sr. very well, as the Michigan State Police post in East Lansing was about a mile from the Frandor Sears location the senior Herr had worked at for over thirty years. These officers would regularly come into the store and buy tools and hardware, and they all thought highly of my paternal grandfather. He was well liked.

The first such witness was Sergeant Paul Brabent, a Michigan State Police crime lab expert. He testified that "the print was made by one palm...and no other palm; the right palm of Richard George Herr." Officer Brabent testified that the print was taken from the knife brought to him in a waste paper basket by detective Keith.

Lieutenant George Hein, a State Police latent fingerprint expert, was the next witness to testify. He stated that "...the palm print on the handle was so clear it was photographed without having to dust the knife." Hein went on to add that it was so clear due to the presence of "...a foreign matter...which I believe was blood." Dust is usually used to bring out fingerprints. The Lieutenant added that the knife was also dusted and several photographs were taken of the print. Hein testified that "a clearly visible print on the handle of the knife matched the area of Herr's right palm near the fingers." Under meticulous laboratory tests, Hein said he found "...at least twelve points of comparison" between the print on the knife and the defendant's palm. Hein then testified that he gave the photos of the prints to detective Richard Brabent who made the actual comparison with the print taken from defendant Herr by detective Keith.

The final witness of the day was Dr. Charles E. Black, a pathologist, who testified that Betty Reynolds died of "hemorrhage and shock." He said that the victim's throat was cut "by slashing...with a comparatively dull instrument...to the bone." He stated that it was a dull instrument because "...neither of the common carotid arteries in the neck were cut as was the esophagus and wind pipe." Eight stab wounds about one inch wide in the chest, one completely through the heart to the back bone, were noted in the autopsy the Pathologist added. Another stab wound, above the left ear, went through the skull but not into the brain Black added. And the victim had another "irregular wound" on the top of the left foot. Dr. Black surmised that the victim lived about "five to fifteen minutes after the throat wounds and placed the time of death as "ten to thirteen hours" before the autopsy which was conducted at 2:00 a.m. the morning of July eighth. The doctor also testified that the wounds were made with the victim lying on her back, her hands tied behind her "when she was still alive." The assailant had hogtied and positioned the victim so that she could see what was happening to her. "No defense wounds were found on the hands" he said, and there were no signs that the victim was raped despite the fact that she was found nude.

The testimony finished at 4:30 that afternoon, at which time Judge Ballard adjourned the examination and scheduled it's completion for the following Monday, August eighth.

Judge Ballard's courtroom was once again crowded to capacity on the eighth, the room was steaming hot with no air conditioning and only a small corner fan provided relief for the over sixty spectators who made it into the court that Monday. The trip to Charlotte for those coming from the Capitol city was tense. That prior evening in Lansing a race riot had broken out between black youths and white agitators, with bayonets and baseball bats being drawn, business windows and automobile windshields smashed, and four being shot in the downtown business district.

The hearing resumed with the Prosecution calling Dr. Edgar W. Kivela of the state Health Department's crime detection laboratory. Dr. Kivela stated that the knife found in the waste paper basket "...very definitely" could have been the one wielded by the slayer and that the stains on the knife were from human blood. He said that he used scrapings from one of the brass rivets of the handle to determine by serological tests the presence of human blood, and that he planned on further tests to determine the blood type. Dr. Kivela testified that the knife was "Very Dull" and that there were wounds on the victim's right shoulder where the knife's edge did not penetrate but caused bruises. The knife was then entered as an exhibit; it was about fourteen inches long with a serrated edge, the type used to slice meat.

The Defense attorney, Leo Farhat, questioned Dr. Kivela about the time span between the autopsy and his analysis of the knife. The autopsy took place in the early morning of the eighth, and the examination on the twenty-sixth of July. The Doctor said that the delay was to allow State Police fingerprint experts to complete their work, a procedure he said was normal. He also added that he was present at the autopsy and that he noticed that Mrs. Reynolds fingernails were extremely short and that he could not secure any substance from them.

The final Prosecution witness at the examination hearing was John Reynolds, the victim's husband. My father sat, hands cupped, unemotional and stoic, facing Reynolds during his testimony. Reynolds, without emotion, calmly answered the questions of Prosecutor Willard Mikesell and then defense attorney Leo Farhat, as he related the events of the day of his wife's death and his relationship with Richard Herr. The forty-four year old Reynolds, the son of a successful Grosse Pointe Banker, testified that he had known Herr for about a year and that they had met "five or six times" at a Lansing nightclub. He said that they also met during their negotiations for a new car when some difficulties were encountered concerning the attachment of a lien on his previous car in the sales contract. The victim's husband said that to his knowledge Herr had not been to his home previously and that his wife had not met Herr during their meetings at the Lansing nightspot. The widower then detailed the day in January when the defendant met his wife while they negotiated the purchase of a new car. Reynolds voice seemed to quaver just once during the testimony, when asked to repeat when he first saw his wife's body after her murder. "At the Estes-Leadly Funeral Home when she was laid out" he said.

Reynolds detailed the events of the day of the murder. He woke at ten that morning and ate a breakfast of a boiled egg and coffee that "Betty" had cooked for him. The husband stated that his wife had been wearing a terry cloth shift when he last saw her on the day of the murder. He left his home at eleven and went to his office at the Chapel Hill Memorial gardens in Lansing. Reynolds testified that he left his office an hour later to conduct business at the Barker-Fowler Electric Company in Lansing. He then went to the Lansing Glass Company and returned to his office around three that afternoon. He said he was told by his secretary that "something terrible has happened at home-go at once." Reynolds said that he immediately returned home where he found "...a trail of blood from the kitchen to the bedroom."

John Reynolds was then questioned about the discovery of the knife, which he found under the kitchen sink the day after the slaying. Reynolds said that he returned home the following morning with a group of friends and relatives to retrieve some clothing and personal items for him and his children. He went into the kitchen to throw something away when he opened the door under the kitchen sink and immediately saw the handle of the knife protruding from the red wastebasket. The knife was one of two that were missing from the rack on the kitchen wall near the stove. The other missing knife has never been located. The knives had been given to Jack as a Christmas present. Reynolds said that he and three others saw the handle immediately when he opened the door to access the wastebasket. Police were notified immediately, as a few were present in the kitchen at the time and noticed it at the same time as Mr. Reynolds. There was a police presence in the home all night long as the authorities had secured the home and were searching the riverbed for the murder weapon. Sheriff Deputies had been gathering in the kitchen all evening and morning for breaks, many smoking and gossiping, unaware that the murder weapon was so near. Detective Keith arrived shortly after the discovery and removed the wastebasket and knife.

Under cross-examination Reynolds answered defense attorney Leo Farhat's questions rapidly and sharply.

The husband of the victim denied he or his wife planned a separation. He said that August fifteenth would have been their fifteenth wedding anniversary.

The hearing ended abruptly, with Defense attorney Leo Farhat telling the court that he had no witnesses to call.

Judge Ballard then announced to the packed courthouse that he was "satisfied that there was probable cause to try Mr. Herr on an open murder charge." He then bound my father over for the murder of Betty Reynolds and indicated that the trial would take place during the fall term of court in Eaton County.

Farhat asked for an early arraignment in Circuit court and he and Prosecutor Mikesell agreed to the date of August twenty-second where my father would face an open murder charge, with the likelihood that the trial would not begin until October.

Farhat requested cooperation from the State Police and State Health Department laboratories to allow for independent analysis of the alleged murder weapon and fingerprints.

Richard Herr sat emotionless throughout the hearings, only bending over to kiss his wife upon entering and exiting the courtroom. My mother sat in the front of the spectators' row where my father would turn on occasion to chat. One of my father's sisters could be heard crying in the rear of the courtroom.

On Monday August 22nd of 1966, 10:06 a.m., my father was arraigned for the Murder of Betty Reynolds in front of Judge Richard Robinson in Eaton County Circuit Court.

Judge Richard Robinson: Mr. Mikesell?

Prosecutor Mikesell: May it please the court, this is the case of the People of the State of Michigan versus Richard G. Herr. Eaton County number three-o-seven.

Examination was demanded in municipal court originally set for July 12, 1966. At the request of Defense Counsel, it was adjourned to August 3rd, 1966- -yes, August 3rd, and completed on that day. And Defendant was bound over to Circuit Court.
The Information charged being an open charge of Murder.

And the information reads:- -

Judge Robinson interrupts: Represented by Mr. Farhat.

Prosecutor Mikesell: Yes, your Honor.

And the information reads: Richard G. Herr, late of the City of Lansing, in the county of Ingham, and the State of Michigan, heretofore, to-wit: on the 7th day of July, A.D. 1966, at the Township of Oneida, in the county of Eaton, one Richard G. Herr, feloniously, willfully, and with premeditation and of his malice aforethought, did kill and murder one Betty Reynolds, contrary to the form of the statute, and against the peace and dignity of the People of the State of Michigan.

Judge Robinson: Mr. Herr, you are represented by Mr. Farhat, is that correct, sir?

Richard Herr: Yes.

Judge Robinson: I see. It's my duty to inform you that you are entitled to a Jury Trial. That means twelve citizens of this county are selected from what we call a panel of jurors—that meaning a group of citizens called under the law for Jury duty - - Citizens of this County. Twelve of them are selected. They are seated over there on your right. Do you see those twelve chairs over there with the green backs?

They are sworn in. The Prosecutor may present his proofs to prove that you have committed this offense, and you may present yours. And the Jury decides whether or not you are guilty of this offense.

Do you understand that?

Richard Herr: Yes.

Judge Robinson: Do you want a jury trial?

Leo Farhat: If the Court please, at this time, on Mr. Herr's behalf, it is our intent to require a Jury trial.

Judge Robinson: All Right.

Under the rule, I believe it's my duty likewise to advise you this: That you have a right to be tried before the Judge without a Jury. Now I'm - - sometimes we get some confusion there. In other words, you don't have to have a jury. You can have a trial in front of the Judge, where the Prosecutor presents his proofs, and your attorney may present your proofs, and the Judge decides whether or not you are guilty of this offense.

Do you understand that?

Richard Herr: Yes, Sir.

Judge Robinson: Do you want a trial before the Judge, without a Jury?

Leo Farhat: At this time, your Honor, it would be our impression that a Jury trial would be required.

Judge Robinson: All Right.

It is also my duty to inform you that if you are found guilty of this offense here - - there are various included offenses - - but, as charged here, it is my duty to advise you that the maximum could be life imprisonment. In fact, I believe it's mandatory if found guilty of first degree murder. Am I right about that Mr. Farhat?

Leo Farhat: Yes, your Honor.

Judge Robinson: Having that in mind, a plea of not guilty will be entered.

I believe - - unless there's some showing to the contrary - - that is without bond.
That's all.

Leo Farhat: Thank You, Sir.

Prosecutor Mikesell: Thank you, your Honor.

My father then stood and turned to my Mother, hugged and kissed her on the cheek, then whispered a quick "I love you" in her ear as he was escorted out of the courtroom. My Mother, six months pregnant with twins, exited the courtroom flanked by her mother and father, as well as her younger sister Linda and attorney Joseph Louisell.

CHAPTER 11

RESURRECTION

"The Lord is slow to anger and abounding in steadfast love, forgiving iniquity and transgression, but he will by no means clear the guilty, visiting the iniquity of the fathers on the children, to the third and fourth generation."

Numbers 14:18
Old Testament

The resurrection of Christ is the foundation of the Catholic faith. We are taught as Catholics that Christ died on the cross in forgiveness of our sins, and that "on the third day he rose again in fulfillment of scriptures", the resurrection. The New Testament states that Jesus appeared to numerous people over the next forty days prior to his ascension to heaven. We are taught that Jesus did this for our salvation and redemption.

Resurrection was also the name of the church I attended as a child, and was the Catholic School I was sent to for the longest two years of my life. After attending public school for kindergarten and first grade, my mother saw the need to send us to private school. Bussing was being proposed in the public schools for integration, and it was unclear where we would have ended up. Although we had walked the few blocks to Bingham Street School, it was suggested that we would be bussed several miles away to Mount Hope School on the south east side of the city. Resurrection was near our home, a few blocks in the opposite direction of Bingham, located on Michigan Avenue.

Resurrection was a well-established parish, led by a popular priest, Father Francis Martin. Father Martin was an honorable and well respected man. He had been asked to visit my father when he was being held in the Eaton County Jail as he awaited his trial, and was turned away on several occasions by deputies before finally being able to meet with him. The good priest was most familiar with who me and my sisters were and our circumstances when we were enrolled into the Catholic elementary school.

Beginning school at Resurrection was a new and scary experience for all of us. Uniforms were now the norm, navy blue slacks and a white collared shirt for the boys, navy jumpers and a white blouse for the girls. No tennis shoes except for gym class. Add to that my Uncle Greg's horror stories about the school, and the knowledge that we would not know anyone and would have to make new friends.

The students at the school were the children of successful businessmen, local politicians, judges and attorneys, doctors, and civil servants such as fire fighters and police men. The type of environment most would think would be good to place their children. In Lansing at that time, who your father was reflected your importance, and to a great extent helped to dictate your future, many of the children would most likely be cast in a similar profession as their parents. If your parents worked for Oldsmobile, the State, City, Hospital or University, there was a good chance that after finishing school that the children would secure similar positions in the same institutions, using the connections and influence that their parents had built. If your parents had built a successful business, the chances were good it would be passed to the children to run. For those who came from a single parent household, chance was that life would be difficult.

Many of the parents who sent their children to Resurrection at that time were very influential in the Lansing community. The playground before school and after lunch was where the social circles were formed and it seemed important to make the "right" friends. You would often see parents arrive with their children and converse, and of course their children would soon become playmates. My mother brought us to school our first day at "Res", but after that we were on our own.

My older sister Dorette was assigned the duty of making sure we found our way to and from the Catholic school every day.

Dorette and Joelle found playmates pretty quickly; Dorette had a confidence and assertiveness to her that commanded the attention of others. Joelle was just a sweet little girl and well-liked by everyone. My sisters were assisted by the fact that most of the girls were playing stationary games, whereas the boys were running around the playground seemingly uncontrollably. Hopscotch, four square, and jump rope is what you would find the girls doing near the garage of the rectory. I hung close to my sisters initially, but it was clear that this was not my place as I wondered throughout the parking lot playground looking for a friend to meet or something to do. After a few days, a boy named Jim and another named Tom invited me to shoot baskets with them. This was the first time I had ever shot a basketball, and it took a while for me to get the hang of it. The aluminum backboards and baskets were affixed to the back of the old brick school building, and we would take turns tossing the balls up, hoping it would fall through the orange ring.

I was initially separated from my twin sister Joelle in the school and placed in a split second and third grade class. The first classmate I was paired up with was another boy named Joe, who was coincidently the son of the barber who cut my father's hair the Saturday prior to his arrest. Joe was a year ahead of me, and was considered the fastest kid in his class. We would spend our break time drawing cars on the classroom floor and started to form a good friendship. Tom, who I shot baskets with at lunch, was also in this class. Unfortunately, I was not the best student at this time and the administrators decided I should be put back with most of the other second graders.

Jean and Janet Masternak were identical twins who had taught at the Catholic school for years, and had a reputation for being strict. Neither of the twins ever married and they lived together in a small home near the Frandor shopping center on Lansing's far-east side. Jean and Janet taught the second and third graders where discipline and paying attention in class was paramount. I was eventually moved from the split classroom and placed in Jean Masternak's second grade class where my sister Joelle was already acclimated. My older sister Dorette was in Janet's third grade class.

The first evidence I saw of the powers and significance of the social circles at Resurrection came one cold fall afternoon at the start of the lunch period. It was customary for students to line up single file leading up to the white washed wooden cafeteria off the playground to get lunch. There were wooden steps that went up about eight feet to the cafeteria entrance, with only a small pipe railing leading up for people to secure themselves. This is where I first saw and learned of the largest and most feared kid on the playground, I will call him Joe Bubba. I was told to stay away from Big Joe, that he once killed a kid when he threw him off the six foot high platform of the cafeteria entrance. Being the newest kid, I was somehow funneled up the line where I finally ended up directly behind the giant. Joe Bubba turned, looked at me, and with a soft friendly smile, said "Hi". Perhaps Big Joe already knew what I was to figure out later, we were both targeted outcasts.

Although Joe Bubba was by far the largest kid in school, it did not spare him from the biting words and names that were hurled at him on the playground by the various groups of boys and their ringleaders. Maynard, the son of a popular district court Judge was one of the main antagonists. The kids would run around Big Joe, taunting him, at times throwing balls at him. Joe was large, but he was also slow. One day one of the name callers got a little too close and the giant got a hold of him and beat him to a pulp, blackening his eyes and bloodying his lip. That was the end of Joe Bubba at Resurrection; rumor had it he was sent to public school, which too many kids at this parochial school was the scariest and worst punishment possible. Joe Bubba was never seen on the playground again. With Big Joe gone, it didn't take long for the good Catholic boys to find their next target. After a few months of school, word had circulated that my father was in prison for murder.

It was early December and the Lansing area had gotten its first good dose of snow. The kids were running around the playground as was typical, and Jim and I tired of shooting baskets so we wondered over to the playground directly behind the church where the bigger kids were tossing a football around and chasing each other around the makeshift parking lot. One of the older kids approached us and asked us if we wanted to play. He knew Jim, Jim's mother was the physical education teacher at the school and he had an older brother and sister who also attended the school. We said sure and asked what the game was.

"Smear the queer!" the boy exclaimed with a smile as he handed me the ball.

I asked, "How do you play?"

He answered, "You run, and you better hope we don't catch you!"

I took off as fast as I could, but I was soon cornered by the chain link fence on Jerome Street where I was quickly tackled and then piled on. Some of the boys would lead with their knee into the ribs. Others would try to push my head into the ground or take free punches. I remember a small smart mouthed kid that was a year older than me, Jimmy, and after I was able to finally free myself from the pile I went after him. The other kids taunted me. This is where I first learned why my Father was in prison.

"Your Dad's in Jail!"

"Where's your Dad?"

"Your Dad is a Murderer!"

"My Dad says I shouldn't play with you."

"My parents told me your family is bad."

"He's a Herr!"

It was clear that I was to be the new target on the Resurrection playground. I was to pay for the sins of my father, as the passage from the Old Testament says.

I found security by hanging out near the rectory, close to where the girls played. The bigger kids didn't come around this area of the playground often, most likely to avoid the watchful eye of Father Martin and the other priests. There was virtually no other supervision on the playground, so to stay safe it was important to hang out where an adult may pass or view the activities from a window.

I wasn't always able to avoid the conflict on the playground, and I quickly learned that the most effective way for me to fight back against large numbers of attackers was to just growl and yell, and to flail my arms and act crazy. Because of my regular conflicts with the other children it wasn't unusual for me to end up in the principal's office. In fact there was a long period that I don't think I went a day without having some sort of conflict on the playground. In class there were definitely trouble makers, but I truly wasn't one of them. Whenever something happened like a burp or whistle, or even talking when the teachers back was to the class, a group of boys would point me out and I would be blamed. I know many of the other students witnessed this, but no one ever stood up for me except my sister Joelle. One day, frustrated with me and convinced I was a bad seed, Ms. Masternak, instructed the other children not to play with me, which prompted a question from my twin sister Joelle, "Can I still play with my brother?" The teacher told my sister that she was the only one who could play with me.

Danger on the school playground wasn't the only peril me and my sisters experienced during our time at Resurrection. One day on our walk home from school, as we made our turn off of Michigan Ave. and onto Clifford Street, Dorette noticed a man and thought he was following us. She commanded Joelle and me to walk faster. As we turned right onto Eureka, we looked back and the man had just turned the corner onto Clifford about a block behind us. We walked even faster until we got to Rosamond Street where we turned and ran as fast as we could to the safety of our house on the next corner. As we glanced back the man was still following us and catching up quickly. We ran into our attached garage where Joelle dropped her book. Dorette yelled at my twin to leave the book and pulled her inside as the man quickly followed us into the garage.   Dorette slammed the door shut and locked it. We had a Doberman Pincher at this time named Evil, and the name was fitting.   The dog barked angrily at the stranger behind the door. The man soon left the garage and tried to peek into the side bay window and front window. Dorette yelled at him with the phone in her hand that she was calling the police.   We never saw that man again, but my father told us after he was out of prison that he once tried to have us kidnapped. I suspect this man had been sent by my father. This was after my parent's divorce, and I am certain that if it were not for the instincts and resourcefulness of my older sister Dorette, we all may have experienced the same fate as Betty Reynolds.

Problems at school and at home were taking their effect on me. In a progress report dated November 5th, 1975, the teacher wrote (I was called Joel at this time, better complimenting my twin sister Joelle's name):

> *"Joel is having real difficulties socially with his peers. However, with the help we've requested, I'm sure he'll improve. Many written papers are done poorly because of carelessness (possibly inner feelings may be causing his frustrations and are being seen in his written work). A real joy to teach!"* - *Janet Masternak*

Janet Masternak and the Resurrection principle Betty Cosgrove James had convinced my mother that I was in severe need of counseling.   My mother took me to see a Catholic Counselor who worked out of the downtown Lansing YMCA. I remember my mom telling me that if I didn't learn how to behave in school I would end up living at the Y with the other losers. I was obviously unaware at the time that this is where my father was

144

living when my parents met. I saw the counselor a hand full of times and he concluded that I was a normal boy who was experiencing a great deal of stress.

The presence of this stress was exhibited in Friday morning Masses where I passed out three or four times prior to school. I twice fell from a standing position, cracking my head on the hard tile floor of the isle. On one of these occasions I hit the floor so hard it broke the skin of my scalp. As I lay there on the floor of the church, blood flowing from my head onto the floor, many of the boys who bullied me on the playground took the opportunity to chastise me once again, this time in God's house. My mother was called and soon arrived and whisked down the street to our family doctor. There Dr. Haynes ran an array of tests on me; I looked like the bionic man with all of the wires and patches attached to me. In the end, they once again found nothing physically wrong; I was a healthy ten year old boy. The fainting was said to be a defensive mechanism to the stress I was experiencing in school.

To separate me from the rest of the class, Ms. Masternak would often send me to detention or the library. I spent a lot of time in the school library at this time. Luckily, the school librarian who lived just up the street on Prospect from us seemed to know that I was not the boy I was being portrayed to be. She took an interest in me almost immediately.

"What do you like to read?" She asked

"Curious George is my favorite" I sheepishly replied

She glanced at a piece of paper that was in front of me where I was doodling war ships having a battle. I would skip a sharpened pencil across the page to simulate the battleships firing at one another.

145

"Is this what you really like?" she questioned

I shook my head yes.

She quickly went to a shelf and returned. "Here, read this, it is about ship battles and heroes"

It was a history book about John Paul Jones. I was hooked. I then read a book about Francis Scott Key and how he wrote the national anthem while on a prison boat during the war of 1812. Then a book about Andrew Jackson. The librarian helped me find and read every book on American history in that library. Then we turned to the encyclopedias, where I would thumb through, read and memorize random facts of history and cultures. I learned quite a bit in that library, and the time I spent there shaped my love for history. I wasn't always in the library however, and would often spend time between the detention room and class room.

After a year and a half of bullying and taunting from classmates, and no support from the teachers or administrators, my schooling started to deteriorate quickly. I knew the teachers didn't like me and didn't want me around. Janet Masternak's displeasure with me is demonstrated in the following progress report from January 23rd of 1976:

> *"Joel does very poorly on written work. Refuses at times to correct errors. Had ripped up a paper in class just the other day because he did not want to correct the paper. He refuses to double-check papers for accuracy. His motor control is very poor and cursive writing is most difficult for him. Joel certainly does need outside (professional) help. I'm most concerned about Joel. I'm most pleased with*

his reading and spelling progress." – Janet Masternak

Despite the problems I was having in the classroom, one of the positive things I took with me from my experiences at Resurrection was my Catholic faith. I have always enjoyed church. At first I think I was drawn to the pageantry and traditions of a Catholic mass. I learned from the sermons, and church was a refuge for me, perhaps the same as it was for Quasi Moto and his Parisian sanctuary.

Like many of the boys my age attending Resurrection during that time, I became an altar boy. The priests seemed to see me differently than the teachers and administrators at the school. I became one of the favored altar boys. This was not the case at first due to my reputation in the school, but eventually I proved to Father Martin and the other priests how reliable I was. If I was scheduled to do a mass, I was always there and ready. I would also pick up masses for others who would be sick or were not available; it wasn't unusual for me to do a couple of masses on Sundays. It was considered an honor to assist a Bishop in mass, and I helped with masses for both Bishops Sullivan and Povish during this time, but most of my masses were with Father Martin.

There was a time that spring when Father Martin was traveling and another priest, I don't remember his name, was watching over the parish. He saw me having problems with the other kids one day at lunch and he took me into the rectory. He sent the secretary to lunch and then we went to his office where he told me to sit down, he then made himself comfortable behind his desk.

The Priest counseled me about my behavior and gestured to a large paddle that was hanging behind him on the wall. He said that he and some of the other Priests and teachers had questioned Father Martin about me being an altar boy. They apparently believed that I wasn't fit to assist with mass at Resurrection. I plead my innocence and tried to explain to him what was really happening, but he didn't want to hear it. He then commanded me to stand up, pull down my pants, and turn around for the paddle. I refused and told him what my Uncle Greg told me to say if a priest was to ever try and touch me. "If you even lay a hand on me, my Uncle Greg says he will come here and beat you to a pulp!" The Priest seemed stunned; he stopped for a moment to gather his thoughts, then yelled back to me in anger "You are no longer an altar boy, I will speak with Father Martin about you when he gets back, now get to class!" He sent me out to the playground where all of the other kids had already gone back to the classroom. I was in tears and I didn't want to go back into the school. If I went home I knew I would be punished. So I ran to my grandparent's house for shelter, the same as I did when Tom had chased me, from Michigan Ave., up Fairview to Lyman drive.

Several years later I believe this same priest was picked up by the vice squad for soliciting homosexual sex and indecent activities at the rest stop off of I-96 near the Okemos exit. I heard after that the Diocese of Lansing shipped him off to a church in another state, I think it was Iowa. He should have been defrocked!

For the next few weeks I stopped serving Mass, although my sisters and I still attended services each Sunday. When I would go up for communion Father Martin would give me a look, and I could tell he was disappointed in me. He saw me on the playground one

148

afternoon and approached me; I hadn't spoken to him since the incident with the other priest.

"How come you have been skipping Mass" he questioned.

"I haven't been skipping Mass Father" I replied. "I have been there!"

"How come you have missed your masses, don't you want to be an altar boy anymore? If you don't, let me know because I can't keep trying to fill your spots at the last moment" the good priest answered.

I then went ahead and told Father Martin what had happened. He wasn't too pleased when I explained to him the way I had spoken to the other priest; he suspended me for another couple of weeks from my altar boy duties and ordered me to say a couple hundred Hail Marys. After that however, for the next few years, even when I was no longer attending Resurrection, I worked every Sunday morning Mass with Father Martin. I also was able and honored to assist with the funeral mass of my Uncle Patsy, the man who was responsible for keeping my parents together.

I have many painful memories from my time at Resurrection. The way I was treated by teachers and many parishioners because of who my father was is not something one would expect from a place of god. Here is where I learned about Christ's sacrifice on the cross so that all sins would be forgiven, yet these people had no forgiveness in their soul. They would have stoned me to death if they could have. To many of them I was a helpless soul, destined for failure.

There were some good people at this church. Father Martin, the Librarian, and the music teacher Mrs. Klein were all good people. I also knew that several of my classmates felt bad about how I was being treated. I also had several relatives who were also members of the Resurrection parish, and I knew they were good people.

I never blamed the church for how I was treated, always holding my Catholic religion close and knowing that it is people that sin; we strive to be what the church teaches us to be, as unattainable as it may be for humankind.

Resurrection Catholic Church on Michigan Ave. in Lansing

CHAPTER 12

THE KNIFE AND PALMPRINT

"Regrets are as personal as fingerprints"

Margaret Culkin Banning

The most damning piece of evidence against my father in the murder of Betty Reynolds was the discovery of a palm print made in the victim's blood found on the handle of the suspected murder weapon, a simple kitchen butcher knife. The knife was found the morning after the murder by the victim's husband, John Reynolds. He had returned to the home early that Friday morning with a few friends to retrieve clothing and incidentals for him and his daughters. The State Police and Sheriff's Department were at the home at this time, officers had been camped out in the kitchen all night long keeping watch and filling ashtrays with cigarette butts. The search for the murder weapon was concentrating on the Grand River with divers searching the river bottom under the assumption that the perpetrator had tossed the knife into the rivers muddy bottom. Mr. Reynolds entered the kitchen and opened the cupboard door under the sink to throw something away when he immediately spotted a bloodied handle sticking out of the wastebasket. Several others spotted it simultaneously, a bloody knife, the murder weapon, protruding from the top of the filled red waste basket.

Detective Thomas Keith was immediately notified, and he quickly arrived to take position of the seven inch blade, which he subsequently handed over to the State Police crime lab. It was felt that if the investigators could find the person whose palm matched the print on the knife handle they would have their man.

In my father's book Inside Outside, he suggests that the detective, Thomas Keith, took multiple sets of fingerprints from him and then transferred the prints onto the knife...but he left out the fact that the image on the knife was imprinted in blood which would make it nearly impossible today, let alone in nineteen sixty six, to transfer a print in blood onto an object such as a knife and have it be so clear. Also, the dusting and photos of the palm print on the murder weapon were taken three days prior to my father's arrest.

The defense attorneys knew that the fingerprint evidence was a large key to the case and to have any chance of an acquittal for my Dad they would have to challenge the evidence to try and minimize its impact on the impending trial.

A Pre-Trial Hearing was held in the circuit court in Charlotte on the fingerprint evidence on October 24th, 1966, where the following occurred:

Judge Robinson: Case of the People versus Richard G. Herr, H-E-R-R, case number 307. Mr. Mikesell and Mr. Zimmer representing the People, and the Defendant are represented by Mr. Farhat and Mr. Louisell.

This is a pre-trial. We've had some conference in my office on this matter. And I wonder if you would make a statement. Did you want anything in particular at this time? - - I think there were some demands made by the attorney for the Defense. Maybe that would be the best way to start.

Mr. Farhat?

Leo Farhat: If it pleases the Court, we were in chambers conferring with the court. The defense advised the court at that time of the status of the case and made a demand at that time, and we renew it at this time on the record, for some photos, copies of all investigative reports which have been prepared, submitted, collated and collected by any police agency which was involved in the investigation of the homicide which this case is connected.

We have further made a demand, your Honor, for a copy of a photograph which our investigator has advised us as being prepared by members of the State Police post. On October tenth I wrote to Mr. Mikesell asking as follows:

> *(Reading)* *"- - One thing that we feel should be done at this time, and which we feel you can facilitate, is a reproduction for our purposes of a blown-up copy of a latent print now in the possession of the Michigan State Police. The reason I am asking for this now is that our investigator who examined the print was informed by members of the State Police that new photos would be taken of the print and would be developed on paper different than the present photo. Detective Hein believed that these new photos will improve the picture so that you will have better evidence. But, when our investigator requested a copy, he was informed he could not receive a copy until they were rendered in evidence.*

We feel it absolutely necessary, to prepare a defense in this case, that this photograph be made available to us as soon as practicable.

Judge Robinson: Then I believe, we'll get to that later, another report. Mr. Mikesell?

Prosecutor Mikesell: If it pleases the Court, as far as this photo is concerned, it has no evidentiary value for comparison purposes at all, as I understand it. It's merely a blow up of the print which would be used by an expert for demonstrative purposes. It isn't that it shows the print; the comparison print is exactly the same as it has been. It's merely a picture, rather than the print itself.

Judge Robinson: Of course, if the original photo is to be taken, I think he would have a right if it is a copy to see if there was a similarity between the two of them.

Prosecutor Mikesell: As I understand, the original is on an inch-by-inch scale which is used for comparison purposes. And the State Police have made a photograph of this print so that it can be seen as you observe it with the naked eye. But it's - - they have only made one, and it's not for comparison purposes. And previously, we have given defense, at their request, the opportunity to send their experts up to the State Police post crime lab and use their facilities to make any comparison they want to make of the actual prints themselves.

Judge Robinson: Well, I'm not quite clear now what you do want, Mr. Farhat. You want what - - a copy of that blown up photograph, is that it?

Leo Farhat: Yes, Sir.

May I respectfully point out also to the court, Mr. Mikesell, in chambers, and he's inferred here today, plans to use this blow-up for purposes of demonstrating to the Judge and Jury the points of similarity between the prints taken from Mr. Herr and the print on the knife. Certainly it escapes comprehension how he intends to do so, unless he plans on offering that blown up photograph as an exhibit.

May I also ask the court at this time to ask the assistant prosecutor to state his position on the record regarding the refusal of the Prosecutor to turn over to us photo copies of the investigative reports.

Prosecutor Mikesell: I would like to speak for the Prosecutor's office on this for a moment before we do that.

Let me say that there has been no motion filed for these reports, and it is our position that some authority should be cited by Counsel. After all, it's their demand. –That some authority should be filed so that we have an opportunity to argue this before the court as to what just exactly Counsel is entitled to know, and what they are not entitled to know, and have a ruling by the court on this. And, until petition is filed, we are not in very much of a position to defend it.

Judge Robinson: may I suggest this. You don't have reports of the examination that you had recently, Mr. Farhat. We are waiting for that. And why don't we adjourn this, say two weeks, and can you have all of your investigative reports here Mr. Mikesell?

Prosecutor Mikesell: Yes.

Judge Robinson: Then we can go into that on that day.

Prosecutor Mikesell: I might suggest at this point, in as much as the matter has come in a round about sort of way, that I'm presently checking the court file and I find no Appearance of any attorneys there for the Defendant in the file.

Leo Farhat: May I respectfully point out, this does not preclude Mr. Mikesell and the court for notifying us as of the hearing of the pre-trial, and I assume the series of correspondence which has taken place in the past at

157

least had inferred that we were here for Mr. Herr. We'll resolve it now and later.

Prosecutor Mikesell: I feel there should be an appearance by – written appearance by all the attorneys representing the Defendant in the file.

Judge Robinson: That can be taken care of by filing them. Suppose we do that, gentlemen?

Do you have a day Mrs. Fowler that we might have something on this matter – a half day somewhere? Two weeks is what?

Mrs. Fowler: November 7th and that's opening day in Barry.

Judge Robinson: All right. I suppose it would be against the law to have it on Election Day, wouldn't it?

Prosecutor Mikesell: Yes.

Mrs. Fowler: We have Thursday morning, the 10th.

Judge Robinson: How about that? In the morning at nine, thirty. –The tenth of November, is that all right? -- Thursday, November tenth at nine, thirty.

It might be well if you filed a formal motion Mr. Farhat.

Could You have your record and your reports in court? Is that satisfactory? --All right.

We'll recess.....

The pre-trial hearing on the palm print evidence continued on November 10th, 1966. Judge Archie McDonald filled in for Judge Robinson.

Judge McDonald: Case of the People versus Richard G. Herr, Case number 3-0-7.

Mr. Zimmer representing the Prosecutor's office, and Mr. Farhat representing the Defendant.

As I recall it, this matter comes before the court by way of a petition – motion for the production of certain records, and so forth. And I believe it's your – State your position first Mr. Farhat.

Leo Farhat: Thank You your Honor. If the court please. The court has stated the substance of the proceedings.

At this time we are asking for the production of certain documents and instruments, including a copy of the latent print; a copy of the blow up of the latent print which the People allege to be that of the Defendant which they had preserved of the handle of the knife found in the Descendant's home by the Descendant's husband following her death.

Judge McDonald: Let the record show that Mr. Mikesell is here.

Leo Farhat: The second thing we have asked for are reproductions or photocopies of the reports, statements or memorandum, investigations and communications, which were prepared and forwarded to – obtained by the Eaton County Sheriff's department from the cooperating police agency involved in this investigation, and one of their other statements and conclusions that may be in the possession of the Prosecutor. Not directly or indirectly given to him by the police agency, but which may be considered as part of the investigation in this case, exclusive of opinions and work products and so forth.

Judge McDonald: Mr. Zimmer?

Assistant Prosecutor Zimmer: If it pleases the court. The people on this matter stand in direct opposition to the request made by Mr. Farhat. He is asking for items that he is not entitled to – some which he is not entitled to at this time.

We feel that unless authority is presented to the court, either by statute, court rule case law of this State, case law of other States, case law of the Supreme Court or the federal courts, indicating that he is entitled to these things, we feel that we should not be made to supply them to him.

I think that what Mr. Farhat is asking for, he's not asking for as a matter of right, but as a matter of privilege. That is, he does not have an absolute right to demand any item from the prosecution at this time, but he is coming into court saying that, "If the court so pleases, may I have these items." That is, the court has absolute discretion to deliver or deny the delivery of these items to him. This discretion however is governed by certain principles, certain statements of law which I think the court should be aware of. And, in my examination of the law on this subject, I find that there are at least five major points that must be satisfied, before the court will grant any production of evidence, documents, statements or other wise to the Defendant –Defense.

The five major points, which I would like to make to the court, are:

That the items that the Defense seeks to be delivered to him must be admissible into evidence. They must be items which the Prosecution can produce at trial and introduce into evidence.

The Defendant, I think, must show that fairness and justice must be denied if these items are not produced to him prior to trial.

And, I think, the Defense must show a compelling necessity for this inspection so that the court may order such an inspection, prior to trial.

I think, also, that the burden – for this entire area of inspection and for the right and privilege to have inspection, is upon the Defendant to show that he must have them; not for the Prosecution to show that they need not produce them for him. I think the entire burden in this area rests with the Defense.

And, finally, your Honor, this type of motion can not be used as some type of fishing expedition; that the Defense cannot come into court and say, "well, we want this information. We want to know what the Prosecution has; what they intend to produce so that we can make a better defense." But, in doing this, the Defense cannot come in with the attitude that they are entitled to these things so they can see what's going on, to fish for loopholes or to look for items they have not discovered.

I think those five things are extremely important.

I think the defense must also show –

161

Judge McDonald interrupts: You say, five? Would you say what those are, again?

Assistant Prosecutor Zimmer: That the items must be admissible in evidence. That it must be shown that fairness and justice will be denied –

Judge McDonald: All right, don't go so fast.

Assistant Prosecutor Zimmer: - if the items are not produced.

Judge McDonald: All right, number three.

Assistant Prosecutor Zimmer: compelling necessity for inspection must be shown.

Judge McDonald: All right.

Assistant Prosecutor Zimmer: The entire burden for the request rests upon the defendant.

Judge McDonald: All right.

Assistant Prosecutor Zimmer: And, that a fishing expedition shall not be allowed. And, I would like to make a comment as to a couple of points which are adjuncts to these five points I have made.

I think the Defendant must come in and show that he is unable to find these items, or to find out the points or to discover the items which he seeks from the Prosecution by his own ability, by his own investigation; or that he will be surprised at trial, or that he will be taken advantage of because the Prosecution will not divulge these items, or similar arrangements along that line.

Now, to deal specifically with the two items asked for, basically two items – police reports and everything that goes with it, and a copy of a latent print, or a blow up of that print, I would like to deal with each one separately.

As far as the people are concerned, the Defense has no right to any Police report, except upon trial, and except for impeachment purposes.

I would like to state on the record, and I don't think Mr. Farhat will object to this; the Defense did obtain at preliminary examination the report of detective Thomas Keith, which was primarily the report made in this case, comprised some twenty or thirty pages, or thereabouts, and it contains a general statement as to everything that was involved on this investigative end of the case. He does have that in his possession now. But, he is now speaking in the way of Police reports, the various means, the reports made by other investigative police officers.

I would like to state to the Court that the authority in this State is that the Defense is not entitled to discovery or inspection of police reports, except upon trial and except upon the condition that the officers who made the report takes the stand and testifies. And then, -- even then the Defense is entitled only to the portion of the report which covers areas which the officer or officers on the stand can testify to. That eliminates all hearsay, all statements of opinions, and all matters which the officer cannot testify himself.

Now, turning to the print, itself, the defense has been offered the use of the State Police crime lab to examine, -- to compare, to observe and to generally conduct any investigation they are to with regard to the comparison of the latent print removed from the knife in question and the known prints of the Defendant, Mr. Herr. I understand that a sort of investigation of this nature has taken place. They have been given the right, and they have sent their representative to examine those prints.

Judge McDonald: I would like to ask a question and maybe it isn't a fair one. Maybe you can't answer it. -- Maybe you won't want to.

I suppose you are talking about fingerprint impressions, are you?

Assistant Prosecutor Zimmer: Yes, sir.

Judge McDonald: All Right. At the time of the trial, I can imagine you perhaps might be going to use blown up kinds yourself, blown up pictures, -- and do you claim they have those?

Assistant Prosecutor Zimmer: I intend to get to that point right now, your Honor.

Judge McDonald: All Right.

Assistant Prosecutor Zimmer: As far as the blow-up is concerned, it is my impression that this blow-up will be an enlargement of the print, and will be used for demonstrative purposes to explain to the court and to the Jury exactly what the fingerprint expert has done with regard to his comparison. In other words, the full print is of such a small size that the Jury couldn't really observe it.

Now, the position of the prosecution on this point is that such a blow-up is in the nature of a visual aid; it's in the nature of a work product of the police and it is something used to convey the truth, it's not the primary evidence. The primary evidence is the print, itself, or the lift that has been taken, and we'll object to the Defense obtaining items which are purposely constructed for demonstrative use, which the Prosecution has reason to believe this blow-up will be used for; and I would compare this to the handwriting analyst or the typewriter analyst who makes the large charts indicating the size of the letters and the slants of the letters and places them in front of the Jury and explains, "Here's how I made the comparison," rather than the actual document or writing or typewriting that is introduced into evidence.

Judge McDonald: Let me ask you this. You say that you have given them access to certain things, and I assume access to see these prints and probably they were used - - were these used in the examination?

Assistant Prosecutor Zimmer: Yes, your Honor.

Judge McDonald: Any objection to their making them themselves, -- making a blow-up?

Assistant Prosecutor Zimmer: Well, I'm afraid I can't speak on that, your Honor, because I don't understand the technical procedures involved in the making of the blow-up. I don't know if they could bring in their own equipment to do it; if the State Police would do it for them. I don't feel the State Police should be made to do it for them.

I understand it's a difficult process, it's time consuming and not easy to do.

As far as their ability to make their own, Mr. Farhat would have to speak on that. I am not familiar with the technicalities involved, and as I have stated, they have offered these prints.

Now, whether or not they are able to make their own blow-up is a question that I really cannot answer, because of the technicalities. I suppose to get a final answer in on that we would have to bring one of the experts in, either our own or the defense expert to testify as to what can be done.

Leo Farhat: May I point out respectfully, your Honor, that the experts relied upon by the People are here, and while the motion is made -- based upon the testimony they offer, I would be pleased to have the court examine one or both of them to inquire into the process, because I am no more expert on this subject than Mr. Zimmer.

Judge McDonald: Well, we - - I anticipate when you get through stating your respective positions of going into my office and discussing this further. Perhaps we can do that in there. Keep these gentlemen here, and we'll see.

Go ahead.

Assistant Prosecutor Zimmer: If it pleases the court. I have one more point to make and that is there is no legal authority in this State for criminal discovery, and I think that honestly speaking what the Defense is seeking in this case is criminal discovery.

I would like to refer the court to General Court Rules of 1963, rule seven, eighty-five point one, subparagraph two, which states - - and this was a new addition in 1963, it was not a carry-over from the old Michigan court rules. It states as follows:

(Reading) "Depositions or other discovery
proceedings under chapter thirty of these rules
shall not be taken for purposes of discovery in
criminal matters..."

And, of course, chapter thirty is the chapter which
controls all the discovery proceedings in the courts of
general jurisdiction of this State.

So, in closing, I will state no authority has been shown
and the burden has not been borne by the Defendant to
obtain these items. Criminal discovery is not available.
If anything is available to the Defendant it is only by
way of privilege. Control of that privilege rests entirely
in the discretion of the court, and this discretion is
bounded by certain standards or rules which the
prosecution feels this court should follow in making any
determination.

Judge McDonald: Do you care to say anything further
on this situation, Mr. Farhat?

--I think we can perhaps-- we can go in and discuss
this.

Leo Farhat: We believe, your Honor, if the court wants
to discuss this in chambers.

*The court is recessed and Prosecutor Willard Mikesell and
Assistant Prosecutor Donald Zimmer join Defense
attorney Leo Farhat and Judge Archie McDonald in
chambers where they meet for some forty-five minutes.*

Prosecutor Mikesell: If it please the court. From our
conversation in chambers, I understand it is the desire
of the Court and the Defense counsel to have testimony

167

as to the process of making these prints and Detective Hine is here to testify.

Detective Hine is called as a witness to testify on behalf of the State, after first being sworn in to "tell the truth, the whole truth. and nothing but the truth..."

Assistant Prosecutor Zimmer: State your full name, please?

Detective Hine: George L. Hine.

Court Reporter: How do you spell that?

Detective Hine: H-I-N-E.

Assistant Prosecutor Zimmer: What is your occupation?

Detective Hine: Detective, Michigan State Police.

Assistant Prosecutor Zimmer: Do you have some type of specialty connected with your occupation?

Detective Hine: I work in the latent print unit, headquarters-- Michigan State Police headquarters , East Lansing Michigan.

Judge McDonald: You work where?

Detective Hine: Latent print unit.

Assistant Prosecutor Zimmer: As you probably realize we are here on a motion in the case of the People of the State of Michigan versus Richard Herr. Have you had occasion to do any print work with relation to this case?

Detective Hine: Yes I have.

Assistant Prosecutor Zimmer: Now, we are here on a motion to have certain documents and certain evidence, certain items produced for the use of Defense counsel, now since I'm not very familiar with the techniques and problems involved with fingerprint analysis, and since we are here to decide what can be done and what can't be done, what can be reproduced and what can't be reproduced?

I would like you to state to the court what items – prints, negatives and pictures, what with regard to the items – prints, negatives and pictures, what with regard to the items in this case, what you have done with them and what other items are connected with them.

If you would do this in your own words I think we can do it much more easily than if I asked you the questions. So would you please indicate to the court what transpired with regard to your activities?

Detective Hine: Yes, Sir.

A knife was submitted to our unit by detective Tom Keith in reference to the investigation of this murder. On the handle of the knife - - upon examining it a print was visible.   The print was then photographed with the use of a Crown photographic camera at our office.

Later – Excuse me, I got ahead of myself.

This camera, when you take a photograph, it's set up so that it's a one to one size. In other words, the image upon your negative is the same size as what your object is.

-- Later I received from Detective Tom Keith, rolled inked palm prints of one, Richard G. Herr. I then examined and compared the print from this negative with the palm print.

Judge McDonald: I might – Might I inject an idea here?

I don't think we are concerned with this as to the authenticity of these things that might be getting into the trial. --Just what you have to do, I think that's what we want.

Detective Hine: This is what I am trying to get to.

Judge McDonald: In other words, I want to be very cautious, we are not trying this case.

Assistant Prosecutor Zimmer: I don't think any opinion testimony is to be introduced here.

Detective Hine: I'm just leading up to it your Honor. -- My original examinations are made then from these negatives, and the actual inked impressions. They are made on a one to one basis.

Judge McDonald: What does that mean?

Detective Hine: Actual size.

Judge McDonald: I see.

Leo Farhat: Excuse me. May I ask this? You say you compared the known print to the negative, Mr. Hine. Is it the reproduction to the negative or the negative itself?

Detective Hine: The negative, itself.

Now, these blown-ups, they are made from the inked palm impressions, and also from the photograph of the print on the knife.

Judge McDonald: Well, you better start back, again, you lost me for a minute. You are given certain things, -- fingerprints, and then you are given actual fingerprints, I take it?

-- known finger prints? And then you take a picture. You might state that over again, I got a little lost what you said.

Detective Hine: Photographs were taken of the print on the knife.

Judge McDonald: All right.

Detective Hine: My comparison was made from this photograph to the actual inked impression. --

Then, for a court exhibit -- we take this original negative, from the knife in this case, and we also photograph the inked impression with -- with these two negatives, we then make a court exhibit. This is just merely an enlargement to show the Jury and the court how that examination is made, what we use in making our comparisons. Often times, they aren't even put in as evidence, these blow-ups. The examination is not made from these enlargements.

Judge McDonald: Well, you are getting into the legal aspects of what transpires in Court right now, aren't you, telling us what they normally do at a trial?

Detective Hine: Well. I may be.

Judge McDonald: To get back to that phase of it which we discussed in chambers, there's been some distinction made by the Prosecutors office that they are not evidence, but they are used to demonstrate -- for demonstrative purposes. It's a little hard for me to distinguish between the two when we go before a Jury.

In other words, if it is used for demonstrative purposes, it's merely to see the original a little clearer, to have a distinction without a -- --

What you do is take the print-- and then you what? -- Take a picture of the print, or-- Maybe –

I'm not a photographer, you can see that.

Detective Hine: No, Sir, we take the photograph we have taken of the object that has the latent print on it.

Judge McDonald: All right.

Detective Hine: We make a comparison from that photograph with the actual impressions that are taken from the persons.

Judge McDonald: Can you do that over again? Is it a big job to make another one?

Detective Hine: It is quite time consuming sir.

Judge McDonald: What do you call time?

Detective Hine: To give you an actual breakdown, I couldn't.

Judge McDonald: Well, approximately.

172

Detective Hine: It would probably take a full day.

Judge McDonald: And, this would be to reproduce the same thing as was already produced?

Detective Hine: Yes.

Judge McDonald: -- And, in possession of the Prosecutor, or in your possession?

Detective Hine: Yes, to reproduce what we have.

Prosecutor Mikesell: May I ask a question?

Would you have any way after you had done that of being absolutely sure and being able to testify that that was an exact duplicate, shall we say, the exhibit and the negative that you would be testifying to?   The negative that you used for comparison purposes?

Would you be able to say that the picture that you would take now, would be exactly the same as the one you used for comparison?

Detective Hine: Well the picture -- or the blow-up would have to be made from the negative that I originally used.

Leo Farhat: Let me ask you, Detective Hine, how many photos did you take of the knife handle. How many negatives do you have in your possession?

Detective Hine: I have several. I don't know the amount.

Leo Farhat: And, you used only one of those? Is that correct?

Detective Hine: Yes, Sir.

Leo Farhat: Have you made a comparison between the one that you ultimately used, and the others that you have already made?

Detective Hine: The one that I used on the exhibit is this.

Leo Farhat: You've advised us that you have taken this one negative and you've compared that with the photograph negative of the known print?

Detective Hine: Not a photograph, -- of the actual print, itself.

Leo Farhat: I'm talking about the known print.

Detective Hine: That's what I mean, -- of the actual print, itself.

Leo Farhat: Oh, you compared it with the actual print?

Detective Hine: Yes, Sir.

Leo Farhat: All right. How many of those negatives of the knife do you have?

Detective Hine: I have several.

Leo Farhat: All right. Why did you select the one that you ultimately used?

Detective Hine: It's better quality.

Leo Farhat: Than the others?

Detective Hine: Yes, Sir.

Leo Farhat: In other words, you then-- you took the best one?

Detective Hine: Yes, Sir.

Leo Farhat: Are any of them comparable quality?

Detective Hine: No, they are either darker or lighter.

Leo Farhat: Does that in anyway affect your ability to locate points of identification on the negative for comparison to the inked impressions?

Detective Hine: It's according to how much difference in shade of lightness or darkness it would be, yes, Sir.

Leo Farhat: In other words, then, by use of negative that you did in fact use, you were able to find more points of identification than you were in the other negatives?

Detective Hine: Yes, Sir. I was going for quality all the way.

Leo Farhat: So that none of the others have the same quality as this one?

Detective Hine: No, sir.

Leo Farhat: Is it possible to reproduce a -- or to make a positive of the negative that you used for comparison, so that it has the same quality for purposes of identification as the negative, itself?

Detective Hine: In each step of photography you lose a little bit.

Leo Farhat: How much would you lose by creation of a positive?

Detective Hine: I don't know, sir.

Judge McDonald: Percentage-wise?

Detective Hine: I can't break it down that way your Honor.

Judge McDonald: All right.

Leo Farhat: So, then you refer to a day for the purpose of reproducing what we have now. You say then it will take you a day to ultimately obtain from your photography a negative of the knife handle as good as the one that you have now, and that from which you made your comparison?

Detective Hine: No, I wouldn't go back to the original handle now no more.

Leo Farhat: You wouldn't?

Detective Hine: No, Sir.

Leo Farhat: Why?

Detective Hine: I would have to work from the negative that I have.

Leo Farhat: Well, could you?

Detective Hine: Since the knife leaving my hands, it's been out of the health lab, gone through many hands.

Leo Farhat: Was not the print itself protected?

Detective Hine: Just merely by a plastic sheet that was in during the time of examination.

Leo Farhat: That wouldn't have preserved it intact so that you could get a better print?

Detective Hine: I don't know if I could get a photograph as good as what I did when I originally had it.

Leo Farhat: Well then this day's process, is the time you would need to make a negative from the negative of what you have?

Detective Hine: Yes, and then make a photograph of it.

Prosecutor Mikesell: Let me ask a question - - excuse me.

How many - - I believe you spoke in reference to the fact that you are in the crime lab, Michigan State Police department?

Detective Hine: Yes, Sir.

Prosecutor Mikesell: How many crime labs such as yours, the Latent Print Divisions are there attached to the Michigan State Highway Department - - of the State of Michigan - - with the Michigan State Police?

Detective Hine: How many latent fingerprint units are there?

Prosecutor Mikesell: Such as yours?

Detective Hine: There's only one.

Prosecutor Mikesell: What types of cases do you in - - and your staff - - or the staff you are with work on?

Detective Hine: In our unit we work with the latent prints and other parts of the unit works with ballistics and tool markings, handwriting, and typewriting.

Prosecutor Mikesell: What types of cases do you work on?

Detective Hine: Myself, I work strictly with fingerprints.

Prosecutor Mikesell: All right, then this means felony cases?

Detective Hine: Yes, Sir.

Prosecutor Mikesell: And, how many cases per year do you work on?

Detective Hine: I can't answer this for sure.

Prosecutor Mikesell: Approximately?

Detective Hine: It would be hard to even put an approximation on it, your Honor. There's some cases where you might work a week or two weeks on one complaint or one case.

Judge McDonald: I think I know what you are getting at Mr. Mikesell, perhaps I can help you.

We are trying to find out if you proceeded to produce the equivalent to the print that the Prosecutor now has and which apparently has been used, how seriously would it impair the process of administration of justice?

How much time would it take?

Detective Hine: To do the complete detail, you could probably do it in a day.

Judge McDonald: Yes, I know, but would it get you so far behind that everything else would be jeopardized, or - -

Detective Hine: No, Sir, not in one particular incident. This would be a precedent set in this one particular incident, and we would probably have to continue doing it throughout the country, - - throughout the state.

Judge McDonald: Well, you might get a Judge like me that might suggest it. I haven't decided it, anyway.

Detective Hine: Actually, our work is no different than a tool mark identification.

Judge McDonald: Let me ask you this question. If someone else went in there, do you permit others to go in and use your equipment?

Detective Hine: The Defense attorney had sent one of his men up there, already, and I gave up my desk to him and gave him my glasses and everything else and offered him all of the photographs that I had.

Judge McDonald: Could he use your equipment?

Detective Hine: He used my equipment right there. I won't allow Him to take evidence outside of my room.

Judge McDonald: What do you think about that Mr. Farhat?

Leo Farhat: Sir?

Judge McDonald: What do you say to that?

Leo Farhat: I say, your Honor, that the investigator that went out there to the State Police reported to me that the officers were very cooperative and treated him very nicely, but nonetheless refused to give him the photos and negatives and the blow-ups he wanted.

Judge McDonald: Well, what I was getting at was if Mr. Farhat sent someone in there to get prints - - to use your equipment, he might take a picture of his own.

Is that possible? - - As long as he doesn't interfere with you and doesn't take them away?

Detective Hine: No, that wouldn't bother - -

Judge McDonald: I see.

Detective Hine: I don't see how he's going to make the photographs right there.

Leo Farhat: Why do you say that?

Judge McDonald: Why?

Detective Hine: All we have is a camera.

Judge McDonald: Where do you do yours? -- Where do you finish yours up?

Detective Hine: We have a photograph laboratory that we go down and work in...in conjunction with them in doing the finished work.

Leo Farhat: It would be then, impracticable for him to come there and try and do this?

Detective Hine: Yes, because you are really tying up two different divisions, two different units.

Leo Farhat: It would be a lot more practical for you to do it, than him do it?

Detective Hine: Yes. We are six, seven months behind, now.

Prosecutor Mikesell: What do you mean you are six months behind now?

Detective Hine: Our work load.

Prosecutor Mikesell: Doing what?

Detective Hine: Other work, other case loads.

Prosecutor Mikesell: What other types of cases?

Detective Hine: Latent prints.

Prosecutor Mikesell: On what types of cases?

Detective Hine: Anything from breaking and entering up to felonious assault.

Prosecutor Mikesell: Murder cases?

Detective Hine: Murder carries precedent in our office, and we do it first.

Prosecutor Mikesell: Do you have any murder cases pending?

Detective Hine: Yes, we do.

Prosecutor Mikesell: How many besides this one?
Detective Hine: Myself or the unit?

Prosecutor Mikesell: The unit.

Detective Hine: About five that I can think of right now.

Prosecutor Mikesell: How many have you processed so far this year?

Detective Hine: I don't know sir.

Judge McDonald: Well, if the court suggests that we would like to have you produce one of those, what would be your attitude then?

Detective Hine: I would have to do it, your Honor. But, like I stated, this could spread out and then it could turn out to be quite a production job in every case. It's time consuming.

Judge McDonald: Well, we've a problem now, appointing lawyers. It's something brand new, so - -

Detective Hine: If we never made court exhibits - - we don't have to make them. Your Honor.

Judge McDonald: I understand that, but you do.

Detective Hine: Yes. Just do it so that the ordinary person may see how that a comparison is done.

Judge McDonald: Well, by that you mean the Jury?

Detective Hine: Yes.

Judge McDonald: Anything further from this Gentleman?

Leo Farhat: No, your Honor.

Judge McDonald: That's all.

Do You have someone else you want to put on?

Assistant Prosecutor Zimmer: May I ask a question?

Judge McDonald: Yes.

Assistant Prosecutor Zimmer: Has the opportunity to examine the original negative, - - the first negative, or the negative you used in your comparison, which was made from the knife handle, the original palm print that you used in your comparison, has the opportunity been denied the Defense Investigator to examine those two items?

Detective Hine: No, Sir, it's not been denied. I offered them to him and he looked at them.

Assistant Prosecutor Zimmer: He did examine them then?

Detective Hine: Yes.

Prosecutor Mikesell: These are the same comparisons, the products you used for your comparisons?

Detective Hine: The same negative, the same ink impression.

Prosecutor Mikesell: And, that's still available for any other expert Defense wants to send up there?

Detective Hine: Yes, Sir, it is.

Leo Farhat: May I inquire?

Judge McDonald: Yes, Sir.

Leo Farhat: Detective Hine, you were present when some investigator was at the State Police Post, is that correct?

Detective Hine: Yes, Sir.

Leo Farhat: Did you review with him the points of identification and so forth on the two comparative documents?

Detective Hine: Yes, Sir, I did.

Leo Farhat: Do you recall how many points of identification you pointed out to the investigator?

Judge McDonald: It seems we are getting into a field where - -

184

Leo Farhat: I know your Honor. I didn't inquire until Mr. Zimmer.

Judge McDonald: Well, I think we better keep out of that. Well, as far as I'm concerned, I've heard enough to make a decision on. Anything further?

Prosecutor Mikesell: Nothing further, your Honor.

Judge McDonald: Well, we've got two or three other matters to discuss a little further. Suppose we step into the office.

Prosecutor Mikesell: That's all.

Judge McDonald: Court will recess.

Judge McDonald, Leo Farhat, Prosecutor Mikesell and Assistant Prosecutor Zimmer confer in chambers and then return to the courtroom where the following occurred.

Judge McDonald: There seems to be three areas that we are concerned with here, maybe four.

Number one, a reproduction of a blow up of certain picture taking. - - It's not stated very well, but that's what you want.

Apparently there's in existence such a blow up. It's not been used, but they want it's equivalent.

It would appear from the testimony that they take quite a few of those in order to get a picture of proper light so they could view it.

185

Then, the other is access to all of the police or sheriff records, or anybody connected with it. Any office connected with it I assume.

Is that correct Mr. Farhat?

Leo Farhat: Yes your Honor.

Judge McDonald: That's two.

Number three, they would like any statements taken by witnesses. Conceivably that might be involved - - a part of the police records, and we have mentioned those specifically.

Are there any other items?

Do you think that covers it, generally?

Leo Farhat: The reproduction of the negative itself your Honor. I don't know if the court mentioned that.

Judge McDonald: And, the reproduction of the negative.

Does that cover what you want?

Prosecutor Mikesell: I have never been quite sure, your Honor, whether it's a reproduction of Exhibit "A" which I believe was the one by one negative print of the knife. I believe that's it. - - If that's what they want, so that these officers are sure, I would like to have that explained.

Judge McDonald: Suppose you do that Mr. Farhat; State a little more specifically on that phase of it, what you want.

Leo Farhat: Based upon the testimony from Detective Hine, this morning, your Honor, I would request a reproduction of the one by one - - one to one negative which they made at the time of the photographing of the knife handle.
Number two: We would want a copy of the blow-up which they are going - - which they have already prepared, as I understand it, and which may be used by the Prosecution as a demonstrative exhibit at the time of the trial.

Judge McDonald: Now, getting back to the witnesses testimony, you say you want a copy of the blow up? That would mean just one further removed from the original?

Leo Farhat: Well, the original blow up, I understand, is taken from two negatives, so that it could be reproduced quite quickly, quite rapidly without much –

Judge McDonald interrupts: You are wanting a picture of the blow up? Is that what you want?

Leo Farhat: Yes, your Honor.

Judge McDonald: Which according to the witness, or somewhere it got into the record, it might not be the exact one, because they are not - - the farther you go from the original, they change a little bit?

Is that right?

There's the man nodding his head saying "yes".

All right, anything else on that?

Leo Farhat: As far as the prints are concerned, no, sir.

Judge McDonald: Well, I think I have the picture. I'll get at it as quickly as I can. Anything further at this time?

The fingerprint evidence, along with many of the police reports were eventually handed over to Leo Farhat. The items were examined by Farhat and his investigator Max Seagraves, and they determined that these items would be very damning to the defense in a trial. The two later shared their findings and conclusions with my father and his father, Richard Herr Sr. It was at this meeting in the Charlotte jail that the idea of my dad pleading guilty to the murder of Betty Reynolds was first discussed.

CHAPTER 13

PUBLIC SCHOOL

"Public schools were designed as the great equalizers of our society - the place where all children could have access to educational opportunities to make something of themselves in adulthood."

Janet Napolitano

For the first few years of our education, my sisters and I attended public school at Bingham elementary. It was a neighborhood school close to downtown Lansing, near Michigan Ave. and Sparrow Hospital, and just a couple of city blocks from the local Junior High and High School I would later attend.

Bingham was the perfect place for me to begin my scholarly journey. My mother would walk the three of us to school in the morning, then pick us up in the afternoon; rain, sleet or snow.

At this time I was still very much reliant on my sisters and was truly unprepared for school. Being assigned to Mrs. Phillips half day morning class with my twin Joelle for my first educational experience allowed me to slowly ease into school. Joelle would have me watch her and she would cue me and help me with answers. At this time, I could not count too high, didn't know my alphabets completely, and still really didn't know all of my colors. I remember getting caught up and confused by green, orange, and yellow. Mrs. Phillips and her assistant Mrs. Lynch, once they realized the problem, would pull me aside during play time and quiz me on colors and letters until I finally was able to consistently identify them correctly. It didn't take long for them to recognize my reliance on Joelle either, as they witnessed her get my jacket and help me put it on, and as she tied my shoes.

"Joelle, let Joe tie his own shoes" Mrs. Philips asked my sister.

"He can't, he doesn't know how" Joelle responded.

"Joe, you don't know how to tie your shoes" my kindergarten teacher asked me.

I shook my head no as I looked to the ground, ashamed of my incompetence.

"You're not going outside until you learn how to tie your shoes" she said.

Great I thought, I will never be able to go out to the playground again. Mrs. Phillips pulled over one of the miniature wooden chairs to the coat area where I was standing and asked me to sit down. She then started to instruct me on how to tie my shoelaces into a bow. While she was doing this, Joelle, reached over and started to zip up my jacket.

"Joelle, what are you doing" the teacher exclaimed.

"I'm zipping up his jacket..." my sister responded.

"Why" asked Mrs. Phillips.

"I always zip up his Jacket, either me or Dorette" Joelle answered.

"Joelle, go to the playground with Mrs. Lynch...Joe is going to learn to tie his own shoes and zip his own jacket" the teacher commanded.

It took me the whole recess, but I finally learned to tie my own shoes and zip my own jacket.

Those early years at Bingham were fairly uneventful as one might imagine. After finishing first grade, my mother transferred us to Resurrection. I am certain my mother thought that sending us to the parochial school

191

would be better for us. As you have read, that wasn't exactly the case. After our two year stint at Resurrection, we returned to the elementary school on Bingham Street.

Back at the public school, I was enrolled in Mr. Milligan's fourth grade class, separated once again from Joelle who was put into Mrs. Strolle's merged 4th-5th grade class. Mr. Milligan was a tall man with curly brown hair. Rumor had it he was once a police officer. He was considered to be a good teacher, but was given the more difficult students because he was able to handle them. I am sure my prior progress reports from Resurrection made me a perfect candidate for his class.

The students at Bingham were much different than Resurrection. It was much more common for kids at the public school to be from a single parent household. We weren't the only ones in the school who had a parent that was in prison either. And whereas there was only one black student in the whole elementary at Resurrection, I had numerous peers in my new school who were African American, as well as Hispanic and Asian.

I immediately excelled in my new environment, shooting to the top of the class. I quickly made new friends and became one of the more popular kids in class. My confidence was building and I started to feel better about myself and who I was. I was haunted a few times in that first year back in public school by the ghosts of my father and my experience at Resurrection. A Lansing School District Counselor, I am sure prompted by the transferred transcripts from Resurrection, met with me a half dozen or so times that fall. I didn't like seeing her because we always met during what was supposed to be recess time, and I didn't think there was anything wrong with me or any need to see her. She soon saw how well I was doing in my new surroundings, and after conversations with my new teacher, came to the same conclusion, feeling there was no need to continue our appointments.

In the first Parent-Teacher conference my mom attended since we had left Resurrection, she was uncertain at what she was going to hear. What she did hear regarding me was unexpected. Mr. Milligan told my mother "Joe is a real asset to my classroom! He is one of those kids who is good at everything; he can do and be anything that he wants to, a doctor, lawyer, or police man. It is all up to him and what he wants." After she arrived home from the conferences, my mother told me what Mr. Milligan had said. It was the first time I ever really felt she was proud of me.

At Bingham I became active in several different activities. I joined the cub scouts where I carved and painted my own car for the pinewood derby...and won! This came as a complete shock to a couple of the kids whose fathers had obviously carved their wooden cars...they had expected to win. I also joined the Bingham Bulldogs basketball team. I made many friends while playing basketball at Bingham that I still maintain today. I was also in the safety patrol as a fifth and sixth grader; an honor that was bestowed on only the better students.

Moving from a parochial to a public school was a successful transition not only for me, but for all of us. Although my sisters didn't suffer the overt teasing and abuse that I endured, they were definitely subjected to less obvious forms of discrimination that they may not have been aware of. At Bingham, we were all accepted for who we were and appreciated for what we contributed to the school.

The next year I joined Joelle in Mrs. Strolle's fifth grade class. It was no longer a split class. Joelle loved Mrs. Strolle who lived around the corner from my grandparents on Groesbeck Ave. Fifth grade was for the most part an uneventful year. We had acclimated to our surroundings. I liked Mrs. Strolle, but was not the fan of hers that Joelle was. I never liked that she regularly preached in class to her students about welfare, social programs and such. In a low income school such as Bingham, where half the kids were benefiting from some type of public assistance, I think it was inappropriate to make children shameful for the position they were in. We were not responsible for our circumstances. I remember her asking me and Joelle on several occasions if our mother was still on welfare and if she was looking for a job. These were questions she should have asked our mother if she was curious, not us.

Despite this one issue, I still enjoyed my time in Mrs. Strolle's class. My self-confidence continued to build at the public school until a spring afternoon in fifth grade gym class. Dodge ball was the favorite game at Bingham Street School, and I considered myself as somewhat of a dodge ball guru. It wasn't unusual for me to dive through the air to catch balls or avoid throws. With the thirty plus kids in our class, I would win the game more than others. I would play recklessly, at time sacrificing my body during the game. We would often play with multiple balls, which was the case on this one particular day. I was the last players left on my team when a ball was thrown towards me. I was concentrating solely on the ball when I dove forward, while in the air someone launched another ball that hit me in the feet....I lost my bearings...my mouth slammed

194

into the tile covered cement floor of the gymnasium, sheering off my front teeth to the nerve. The pain was instantaneous, with blood and floor fragments mixing in my mouth.

I was immediately rushed to the office where rags packed with ice were liberally applied to my mouth. My mother soon arrived and rushed me to my cousin Mark, who had a dental office off of Ionia Street in downtown Lansing. My older cousin performed two emergency root canals on my front two teeth. After several visits, Mark had fitted me with a couple of porcelain crowns. I have always been embarrassed by my teeth and mouth after that incident, never smiling with my mouth open.

In sixth grade, Joelle and I again shared a class, the sixth grade class of David Fox. David was the brother of George Fox, who was known for being Magic Johnson's High school basketball coach across town at Lansing Everett High. Mr. Fox was probably the most popular teacher at Bingham. All of the kids loved him and wanted to be in his class by the time they reached the end of their grade school experience. He had a knack for mixing music, literature and theatre, making learning fun. Dorette had been in Mr. Fox's class the year prior and she loved him.

Early into the year I had an encounter with Mr. Fox that shows what kind of a teacher he was. We were split into reading groups and someone from our group started to whistle. Mr. Fox asked for the whistling to stop, but the whistle came again. Mr. Fox approached our group and grabbed me by the arm and pulled me away, suspecting that I was the culprit. I think I laughed when the second whistle came. At that moment, in my mind I went back a few years to the days at Resurrection where I was continually blamed for things I didn't do. I lost my temper and pushed Mr. Fox into and onto a desk, crying and yelling at him. He was shocked by my response and surprised by the strength I exhibited, most likely fueled by adrenalin. He calmed me down and I told him "it wasn't me, I can't even whistle," a fact that Joelle quickly confirmed. Another student sheepishly admitted to the deed, something the good Catholic boys at Resurrection never would have done.

Mr. Fox then took me out into the hallway and spoke to me as an equal. He apologized to me, but told me that I needed to learn to control my anger. That it will only hurt me if I continue to react the way I just had. That I was too smart and too talented to react in that manner; it would affect me negatively in the future. That talk probably changed my life, and changed the way that I approached problems and conflict.

I went on to have great success in Mr. Fox's class. I entered the Lansing School District's Calibury Book contest, and wrote and illustrated a book that was chosen to represent Bingham School in the city wide competition. I also won the lead role in the sixth grade play as James, in James and the Giant Peach. It was a wonderfully arranged play mixing music from James Taylor, the musicals Oliver and Porgy and Bess into Roald Dahl's fantastic tale.

My public school elementary experience was completely opposite of what I endured at the Catholic School five blocks away. As I entered Junior High, I was reacquainted with many of the same kids I had been tormented by at Resurrection. But things had changed. We were now in a public school which probably scared some of them initially, and I was not the same person they knew three years earlier.

As I grew and matured, I started to become my own person and the shadow of my father's crime started to fade. My peers began to judge me through my own deeds, and my own accomplishments. I was starting to use my mind and body to gain success. In Junior High I was a member of the equations team, a competitive math team. I also won six varsity letters in Junior High in track, wrestling, and football.

In High School I excelled at distance running and won five varsity letters in Cross Country and Track, being voted twice captain of the Cross Country team and most valuable runner once. In track I was selected as a Captain in my senior year. I was a good student also, although I rarely studied. My grade point always hovered around a 3.0, and I was fine with that as I typically just coasted through my college prep courses. Without studying, I even scored a 27 on my ACT placement exam for college. A few of my classmates even thought enough of my intellect to try and cheat off of my tests.

In high school I suddenly became seen as the quiet, shy kid. Not that I was not social. I would hang around my friends, listen and observe. One friend even confronted me one time and asked "You hear and see everything, don't you?" I did, but I wasn't a rat, and always kept what I saw and knew to myself. I may not have participated in many of things that went on around me, but my peers felt comfortable with me around.

I was confident in myself and my abilities, and knew and got along with all of my classmates, no matter their background. Even those that I knew at Resurrection saw me differently. I was no longer getting into fights or running away from problems. I had become a bit of a square. I have never smoked a cigarette or marijuana to this day. I also never experimented with alcohol as a minor, although there were many opportunities, and a degree of peer pressure. I would attend the many high school "keggers", having brought an ample supply of ginger-ale to fill my glass. It looked like beer, and the only ones who knew the difference were my close friends and sisters. I was almost busted a few times when a co-ed would ask to have a sip from my glass, I was so ignorant about girls at that time, I didn't realize that the request had nothing to do with beer.

For me, my public school experience was the great equalizer. My father's history rarely came into question, and on the few times it did, it was quickly dismissed. It allowed me, the son of a convicted murderer, an opportunity to have success that paralleled, and even exceeded, the accomplishments of many of my peers from the Resurrection years. One of the main reasons I like to attend the Resurrection Ox Roast during the early fall is not only to enjoy the beef sandwiches or oxtail soup (both of which are really good!); the reason is to see people from those times and to show them how wrong they were about me.

Joseph Herr (striped shirt) playing James in the
Bingham Street School 6th grade play,
James and the Giant Peach in June of 1979

Joe Herr Running in a Cross Country meet in October, 1984

CHAPTER 14

A DEFENSE OF INSANITY

"There is a pleasure, sure, in being mad,
which none but madmen know!"

John Dryden, **Spanish Friar**,
Act II, Stanza 1.

The Insanity Defense in the legal trade is considered the "defense of last resort" and is successful in only about 1% of all felony murder trials. This defense can only be used if it can be shown that the defendant's mental state was such that they could not distinguish that their conduct was wrong. If successful, this defense can stop a trial. This was a strategy that was beginning to be considered for my Father as the evidence against him continued to become clearer.

On October 17th, of 1966 in the Circuit Court room before Judge Archie McDonald, the following occurred regarding this strategy. Robert Luoma was filling in for Leo Farhat on behalf of my father.

At 9:51 O'clock A.M.

Judge McDonald: All right, Mr. Mikesell, - - Who is the moving party here?

Robert Luoma: The Defendant is the moving party you're Honor.

Judge McDonald: And what is it you want sir?

Robert Luoma: Pardon me, your Honor?

Judge McDonald: What was it you wanted?

Robert Luoma: Your Honor, this is a Petition to this court in the matter of the People versus Richard Herr for an order ordering the Sheriff of Eaton County to transport Richard Herr to St. Lawrence Hospital, in the City of Lansing, for the purpose of an electroencephalogram.

I'm here on behalf of Richard Herr, and I have discussed this matter with both Dr. Casey and Dr. Tanay, who made a preliminary psychiatric examination of Richard Herr, and they have both recommended that an electroencephalogram be taken of Mr. Herr.

Judge McDonald: The petition is for transportation?

Robert Luoma: Transportation, your Honor.

Judge McDonald: Any opposition Mr. Mikesell?

Prosecutor Mikesell: No opposition. I think both elements are involved, the Petition taking, and the Order granting.

Judge McDonald: Petition is granted

Thus the matter was concluded at 9:53 A.M.

The first talk of an insanity defense in my father's case came from Joe Louisell, one of my father's early attorneys. My grandfather had hired the nationally known attorney out of Detroit to represent my father. Louisell had become famous for representing Alex Karras in the early sixties against Pete Rozelle and the NFL over the player's suspension for gambling. The Italian American attorney also was known for his work for Detroit's organized crime families. Joe initially believed my father.

Louisell once told a pool of reporters that my father had an "Indestructible alibi," that on the day of the murder my father "was working at an automobile sales lot in Lansing." He added that during the course of his work Herr had crushed his finger and that at the time of the killing Herr was at a doctor's office in Lansing having his injured finger treated. The attorney added that my father's finger was fractured and it was necessary for the doctor to use both bandages and splints. Louisell then told the reporters that the doctor would testify on my father's behalf at the preliminary examination and that the charges against my dad would soon be dropped.

The Detroit lawyer soon became more familiar with the evidence against my father however, and realized that my dad's story didn't add up. He soon came to believe that my father had committed the murder. Louisell decided to have my dad examined at the Charlotte Jail by a Dr. Tanay, a psychologist. The doctor's diagnosis was that my father was a sociopathic schizophrenic.

Hearing the psychiatrists diagnosis and knowing the evidence against my dad, Joe told my grandfather that he would represent my father on an insanity defense but that my grandfather shouldn't waste anymore of his money on his services if my father was to maintain his plea of not guilty; "... Your son-in-law is guilty" he told my grandpa, "...he did it."

With the mounting physical evidence against my father, the inability of the defense team to verify my father's whereabouts for the hour and fifteen minutes around the time the murder, a defense of insanity was being strongly considered by his attorney. It was thought that it may be my father's best chance since his alibi could not be substantiated.

Leo Farhat and his investigator, retired Lansing Police detective Max Seagraves, discussed the strategy with my dad. Seagraves asked my father about a stabbing back in 1959 in Lansing that he had been a suspect in and Max had investigated while a detective with the LPD. A woman on Pine Street in downtown Lansing had a "come one come all" party one Saturday evening. Later, in the early morning, when the party was over and everyone had gone, someone rang the host's doorbell and when she answered they plunged a pair of scissors into her stomach. The scissors had belonged to the victim and must have been taken from the home during the party. Richard Herr was at the party that evening and had been interviewed by the State Police about the incident. My dad confessed to his attorney that he was the one who stabbed the woman on Pine Street that morning. The defense team felt that they could use my father's confession to this crime to help bolster the insanity defense.

My mother didn't like the idea of agreeing to any type of plea, especially one of insanity. Even if it meant that my father would most likely only spend a few years in a mental institution, the stigma of such a confession was simply unacceptable, for it would also be an admittance of guilt, that he was the one who committed the crime.

After my father confessed to the murder of Betty Reynolds, he looked high and low for the best lawyer he could find to help with an appeal. He had my mother search out an up and coming noted attorney from Boston named Francis Lee Bailey, he went by F. Lee.

The now famous attorney agreed to see my father and review his case. My mother picked Bailey up at the Lansing airport and drove him to the prison in Jackson where the barrister discussed the case with my father and mother, and the possibility of representing my dad in an appeal. They gave him a set of court documents and transcripts.

After meeting with my parents, Bailey then traveled to Okemos Michigan where he was to meet with my father's parents. He discussed the case with them and told my paternal grandparents that he was pretty sure he could get my father out of prison, and at least get him a new trial, but it would be on a technicality, and my father might want to consider insanity as a defense. After listening closely to the Boston attorney, Richard Sr. told F. Lee Bailey that he didn't want his son to get out of jail on a technicality, he wanted him to get out only if he was innocent. Otherwise, he was where he should be.

F. Lee Bailey had become famous in November of 1966 from the Sam Sheppard Case where he helped acquit a physician who had been convicted of murdering his wife. The case was the inspiration for the television series, then movie, The Fugitive. He would go onto representing other infamous clients such as the Boston Strangler, also known as Robert DeSalvo, Patty Hearst, and he was part of O.J. Simpson's dream team. F. Lee Baily never ended up representing my Dad however.

During the initial trial it was decided by my father and his defense team that a guilty plea was to be presented to the prosecution for consideration before an insanity defense became an option. After the prosecution and court accepted the plea of guilty, it made no sense for my father to pursue a defense of innocence by reason of insanity as an option for appeal. He had already made a confession to the crime, and as I mentioned earlier, my mother was absolutely opposed to the thought of pleading insanity, especially at that point.

Noted Detroit Defense Attorney Joseph Louisell

F. Lee Bailey (1966)

A Post Card from the 1960s of St. Lawrence Hospital,
home of Lansing's mental ward

CHAPTER 15

SERVING TIME

"He that is taken and put into prison or chains is not conquered, though overcome; for he is still an enemy."

Thomas Hobbes

Twenty five to forty years, that was the sentence that my father was given for his plea of guilty to murder in the second degree. Had he not plead guilty and been tried and convicted of the original charge of first degree murder, my father would have served a sentence of mandatory life in prison without the chance of parole.

Jackson Prison in the late sixties and early seventies could have easily been confused with any U.S. military barracks of that Vietnam era. The population of the penitentiary was mainly younger uneducated men with a disproportionate amount of the population being African American. There were no uniforms, the inmates wore slacks and shirts, and if you took away the guard tower and the barbed wire the yard could at times be compared with a small all male college campus, complete with library, pool and tennis courts.

As was the case on college campuses across the country in the late sixties, drugs were also prevalent behind the prison walls. They were often snuck in embedded in book bindings or in the case of acid, eye dropped onto the pages of books and magazines.

The prison had a newspaper, *The Spectator*, for the prisoners as well as a closed circuit television station. It was often said, and occasionally written, that Jackson Prison, the largest walled prison in the world at the time, was some-what of a "country club" with nearly six thousand inmates. The cells were small, but convicts were allowed personal television sets in their quarters as well as coffee makers.

There were plenty of activities to keep the convicted occupied. There was an activities room that included pool tables, and there were plenty of happenings such as softball leagues, tennis leagues, football leagues, and basketball leagues that were organized and supervised by the prison; trophies were even awarded to the seasonal champions. I remember the many times I entered the prison as a young boy, walking down the long corridor to the visiting area with the tall ceilings and shining terrazzo floor, passing by the long glass trophy cases along the hall way and being mesmerized by all of the shiny brass and silver plated statues with football, baseball, and tennis players. Some of the trophies were surprisingly large. My father would often tell me on my way out after a visit to look for a particular trophy he or his team had won. It wasn't the trophies that impressed me however, what me and my sisters enjoyed and looked forward to most about the prison were the vending machines and the visiting room guard who always presented us with a sucker when we arrived. I would always get cheese and crackers from the vending machine.

Outside live entertainment was often booked and brought in to perform in the large auditorium for the benefit of the prisoners. Several national acts such as Mitch Ryder and the Detroit Wheels, metal bands like Savage Grace as well as local bands like The Third Power and Wilson Mower Pursuit played at the prison after performing in charity concerts in Detroit and Ann Arbor for John Sinclair, a Jackson inmate who was serving a ten year sentence for marijuana possession.

My father states in his book that Sinclair was given the same sentence as himself, 25-40 years, by the same judge for marijuana possession. This is just another of the many untruths and exaggerations in my fathers tale. Sinclair was not sentenced by Judge Robinson in Charlotte, he was sentenced in Detroit by Judge Robert Colombo, and although given a harsh sentence of ten years for his crime of selling two marijuana cigarettes, it wasn't 25-40.

The inmates also enjoyed weekly movies.

It didn't take long for my dad to work his way into many of the prime jobs in the prison. He became the photographer, then editor and artist for the prison newspaper, *The Spectator*, which gave him access to many luxuries and opportunities that were not afforded to the average inmate. How he was able to obtain such a prized position in such a short time behind the southern Michigan prison walls is not known, one can only speculate. He was given his own office in the prison to go along with his cell.

He would also host a closed circuit television show for the inmates called "The Chair" in which he would interview various prison officials and inmates, discussing numerous topics that were important to the convicts at that time.

My dad was able to make friends quickly behind the prison walls. One of his closest friends was fellow convicted murderer Floyd "Butch" Tisi who was also serving a life sentence for stabbing and killing his wife's best friend in 1967. The Judge who tried my father's friend once said of Tisi and his crime... "Even God will never forgive him of this". Tisi's freedom was a strong subject in the United States senatorial election of then MSU trustee Debbie Stabenow as she challenged the Republican incumbent Senator Spencer Abraham. Stabenow was lobbying for Tisi's release, and Abraham was opposed.

He also befriended noted Detroit Mafia kingpin Vito "Billy Jack" Giacolone while the two served time together within the walls of the Southern Michigan Prison. Vito was a grandfatherly looking, stocky and rotund man who once saw me in the visiting room as a toddler and had me bounce on his lap. That was the only time in my life that I have ever knowingly came in contact with a Mafia figure, through my father while visiting him in prison.

In his book, my dad over and over made the accusation that my grandfather, Paul "Harry" DeRose, was a made member of the Detroit mob. This is simply untrue! My grandfather definitely looked the part, and with some of his life choices, even acted the part. He was a slick dressed, handsome Italian man who liked to gamble, owned a strip club, and was hard headed with a bit of a temper. The fact of the matter is he was addicted to gambling and lost much more money than he ever made at the track or playing cards; he nearly bankrupted himself a couple of times betting on the horses.

When his club Amedeo's burnt down in the early sixties it was initially rumored that it was set ablaze for the insurance money, that is what a lot of people believed, and then prosecutor Leo Farhat was eager to pursue charges against him. The truth however was that the nightclub was uninsured and my grandfather had to borrow money from his father-in-law to rebuild it. This is not a mistake a mobster would make; a mobster would have been heavily insured, torching the business purposely. The Amedeo's fire almost ruined him, but my grandfather was resilient and an exceptional businessman; as much as he blew his money on the ponies, he always knew how to make money.

Of course, no charges were ever brought against my grandfather for the Amedeo's fire because no crime was ever committed, at least not by him. It is thought that

212

union musicians set the club ablaze because my grandfather used only non-union musicians. This theory was unfortunately never pursued by officials who were more than pleased that the business was now closed. With a large loan from his in-laws, my grandfather quickly rebuilt his business however, and paid back the loan in a few months.

There are many points that demonstrate that my grandfather was not a member of the mob. Harry DeRose didn't like to share his money, and as a member of the mob he would have had to have shared his earnings, or else. My grandfather and his family were Calabrese, not Sicilian, so to my understanding he couldn't have been "made". As I learned in the movie *Goodfellows*, only those who were 100% Sicilian can be "made". The fact is my grandfather detested the "gangsters" he would see at the track. They were jerks and the stereotypes they fostered only made his life difficult.

My grandfather was also thoroughly investigated by the FBI due to the controversy over his topless bars and well documented battles with then Ingham County Prosecutor Leo Farhat, and later former Lansing Mayor Gerald Graves. There was never any evidence that my mother's father ever did anything illegal, and he was never arrested or tried for anything. My grandfather knew the laws, and would often test them, but he never broke them. Unfortunately prejudices are fueled by stereotypes, and my grandfather looked the part. But he was not a gangster, just as every young black man today wearing baggy pants and wearing large amounts of jewelry isn't a drug dealer.

My father however had no problem with organized crime, and seemed to embrace it while in prison, whether it was the Italian Mafia or the Black Mafia, the Black Panthers or the White Panthers. He would use his position at *The Spectator*, which allowed him access throughout the prison, to help run the gambling and drug trade within the cement walls. He even tried to get my mother to help him smuggle in drugs, asking her to hide them in the bindings of books. He states in his book that he "...was making more money in those days than I did in the free world."

As my father served his time he was no different than many other cons facing a long sentence, spending a great deal of his spare time working on an appeal to his conviction. For years my father wrote daily letters pleading for a new trial. He wrote to Frank Kelly, the Michigan Attorney General. He wrote to U.S. Senator Philip Hart as well as to U.S. Congressmen Charles E. Chamberlin. He wrote to U.S. District Judge Thadeus Machrowicz and to the trial judge who sentenced him, Richard Robinson. He wrote to Michigan television personalities such as Lou Gordon and to the Michigan Bar Association, and even the A.C.L.U. In his letters he always proclaimed his innocence and stated that he had been denied his constitutional right to a trial and denied his civil rights. He would receive responses to his pleas, never receiving the answers he was seeking, and he would then resubmit his requests, over and over and over.

One of my favorite responses to my father's pleas came from the executive director of the Michigan branch of the American Civil Liberties Union, Ernest Mazey. His reply to my father read:

Mr. Herr,

214

I have enclosed a copy of your letter dated March 27th, in which all you related to us was a complaint about your attorney. Again, I reiterate if you have a complaint about him the remedy is the one that you have pursued through the State of Michigan.

Our "Department" as you call it is not a department at all. Our organization is a voluntary association of people concerned with constitutional rights and civil liberties. Our lawyers work without fee only in those cases presenting serious, clear cut violations of such rights. Because of the nature of our organization, it is not possible for us to even consider involvement in every case containing such violations. We, or rather the Board of Directors bases it's decision on how many people would be involved if a change in the law were to occur because of our intervention, as well as the nature of the violation.

If you would care to relate how you got to Jackson without a trial, we would at least have something upon which to make some preliminary determination in your matter.

The last sentence is the one that I find most amusing. My father has always insisted that he was convicted without a trial and was railroaded by the system. He never mentions the fact that he pled guilty after ten months of hearings in his case, having been exposed to all of the evidence against him. Instead he tells his readers that he was held in solitary confinement in the Eaton County jail with no idea of what was happening with his case. Of course, in his book he states that he never saw the evidence against him; he must have been knapping during his arraignment and the several evidentiary hearings?

My father wrote to many famous attorneys, trying to silicate their help in his appeal. He first tried Melvin Belli, the California attorney of the stars, but he was unavailable. Then he tried Percy Foreman, the famous African American attorney out of Dallas, but he was too busy to handle the case also. He then reached out to F. Lee Bailey, who as you read earlier agreed to review my father's case, but never did represent him.

None the less, with the persistent help of my mother, backed by the financial help of my grandfather "Harry" DeRose, my dad was able to get back into court and have a hearing in front of the same judge who sentenced him, Richard Robinson, on Monday February 26th of 1973.

My grandfather this time hired Theodore Albert out of Ironwood. Ted was a brilliant attorney who practiced constitutional law and had represented my grandfather on several occasions against the City of Lansing on Freedom of Speech issues concerning the topless bars. He and my grandfather were also good friends, and Ted would often stay at my grandparent's home when in town. The barrister's strategy on my father's defense included two different approaches. The first was to challenge my father's guilty plea on constitutional grounds in an attempt to get him a new trial. There was a recent United States Supreme Court decision, Boykin v. Alabama, in which the court determined that a defendant must be advised of his constitutional rights against compulsory self incrimination. The hope was to have this new ruling applied retroactively to my dad's confession and the court's acceptance of his plea. The second approach was to get Judge Robinson to vacate my father's guilty plea on the grounds that it was coerced, thereby paving a way for a new trial. Donald Zimmer, who was the assistant prosecutor at the time of the original trial, was now the Prosecuting attorney representing the People.

Leo Farhat was the only witness called to the stand by the Prosecution. At first he refused to testify, exercising the Attorney-Client privilege that he wished to protect. Circuit Judge Robinson ruled however that by the nature of the hearing, Richard Herr had waived the Attorney-Client privilege and that Farhat should answer the Prosecutor's questions. At one point Eaton County Assistant Prosecutor Chester Sugierski asked the well known former Ingham County Prosecutor "Did you coerce Herr into pleading guilty to first degree murder?" The answer was "no."

My father was the first Defense witness called to the stand and he immediately blamed his former attorney, Leo Farhat, of not preparing an adequate defense for him, and then pressuring him into pleading guilty to second degree murder. "At first, Farhat said we had a good case to prove my innocence. Then, about five months later, he talked me into using temporary insanity as a defense. Then, about two weeks before my arraignment on February 20, 1967, Farhat started pressuring me to plead guilty to second degree murder. I objected strongly, but he and his investigator, Max Seagraves, several times met with me and told me I had to plead guilty, one of them was on each side of me, pounding my knees and chest and all that was missing from the third degree treatment was the bright light." My father went on to add that after serving eight and a half months in solitary confinement in the Eaton County Jail, he was in a frame of mind to plead guilty to anything to get out of the county jail. He then added: "Farhat told me he'd quit if I didn't plead guilty. I had already paid him $17,000, and being scared- left out in the cold and ignorant of the law – I felt I had no choice. He and Seagraves kept telling me that seven years in prison was a lot better than a life sentence which is what I'd get if I didn't plead guilty."

My father ended his testimony that Monday by stating that Farhat helped him concoct a story to tell Judge Robinson when he pled guilty adding "He had to. I don't know what went on out there in Grand Ledge on that day." He also stated that some of the persons who could have substantiated his alibi were never contacted by Farhat or his investigators.

My mother also testified at this hearing on behalf of my father. She answered Prosecutor Sugierski's questions and substantiated my father's claim that he had been pressured into pleading guilty. She stated that this is what led her to seek out a second attorney, Evan Callanan, to fight for his innocence.

In addressing the court, Ted Albert informed Judge Robinson that "We also have a case pending in the Michigan Supreme Court maintaining that Herr had not been advised of his rights against self incrimination when he entered his plea. And if he gets a full blown trial, I believe we have a meritorious case which will prove his innocence and will also include a strong allusion to the party who actually committed the crime." Judge Robinson adjourned the hearing, which was to resume on Friday, March 9th, so that Leo Farhat could again testify and provide more information as to the claims made by my father.
The hearing resumed that Friday with the well-known Lansing Attorney answering questions from Eaton

County prosecutor David Smith. Farhat started his testimony proclaiming that he didn't appreciate being put into the position of testifying against a former client, and he denied that he had ever pressured Richard Herr into pleading guilty. He later added that he had been practicing law for nearly twenty one years and testified emphatically that he had not helped my father make up the confession he told the court in order to convince it of his guilt.

Farhat testified that after a private agency he had hired confirmed the State Police findings of Herr's palm print on the murder weapon, Herr finally admitted his guilt. "It was a meeting in the Charlotte Jail of Herr, Myself, Herr's Father and my investigator Mack Seagraves, when Herr first admitted in front of his father that he had killed Mrs. Reynolds. That was after January 9th, 1967 and before the first week of February."

During the course of Farhat's testimony he addressed several of my Father's accusations:

- The Defense Attorney testified that he had never pressured my father into pleading guilty and had never laid a hand on him except to shake hands or when he placed his arm on my dad's shoulder.

- He testified that my father never requested a lie detector test.

- Farhat stated that he had made all investigative reports available to my Father except a psychological examination report that the Psychiatrist advised him not to divulge to his client.

- Farhat said that a thorough investigation was conducted in an effort to support my father's alibi that he had been at the doctor's office at the time of the slaying, but there was a one hour and fifteen minute window that could never be accounted for.

- The former Prosecutor turned Defense Attorney testified that he had visited Herr twenty to twenty five times before sentencing, he had discussed various reports with my father, and had explained the difference between first and second degree murder.

Farhat was often passionate and emphatic during his testimony, obviously bothered and insulted by the nature of the proceedings. My father on the other hand was quite pleased with what he had accomplished, and his glee was captured by a Lansing State Journal photographer as his smiling face, full of delight, graced the front page of the following day's paper.

The hearing approached its conclusion and my dad once more took the stand and proclaimed that he was totally innocent of the murder and had no knowledge of the details of the slaying. He again made the claim that he had been pressured into pleading guilty, although He knew he was innocent, contradicting his former defense attorney's testimony.

Ultimately my father lost in his attempts for a new trial, which was probably best for me and my sisters. The specter of such a trial while we were of school age would have had lasting effects even worse than what we were experiencing.

It is important to note the differences in my father's story during this hearing and the one he tells in his book. At the trial in 1973 my father testified that he was not in Grand Ledge the day of the murder. However in his book *Inside Outside*, he admits to being at the Reynolds home that day in the first few pages.

After the hearing, my father returned to his prison home in Jackson where he resumed his art career, improved on his tennis game, and took the opportunity to earn a degree from Wayne State University.

He was also able to get all of the dental work he required courtesy of the great State of Michigan. I am certain there were difficult and scary days in prison for my father. There were a few incidents of unrest and a couple of riots while he was incarcerated, but overall I think that my father in reality enjoyed prison. When you read his book it is easy to detect the fond memories he holds of his days behind the barbed wire and brick walls of the Southern Michigan Prison. He speaks as fondly of his days there as some may speak of their college days. He made lifelong friends in prison, many that he still maintains today. He was someone inside those walls. He was important. With his position as the Editor of the prison newspaper as well as being the Institutional Photographer and one time commentator of "The Chair", my father had direct access to the Warden and prison staff, and also had the ability to freely move around the prison and make excessive amounts of money moving drugs. He had become someone inside those cement and steel walls in Jackson. On the outside, he is an ex-con, a confessed and convicted murderer who just happens to play Santa Claus every year for thousands of children in Flagstaff, Arizona.

Herr Family Picture taken in Jackson Prison in 1972

Artist Richard Herr in his Prison studio (February 25, 1969)

Richard Herr drawing in his prison cell

Richard Herr interviewing Warden Krupp on the Jackson Prison
closed circuit television show "The Chair"

* * * * *
VING MICHIGAN, THE
TED STATES AND EUR-
: WITH NEWS FROM
WORLD'S LARGEST
LLED PRISON.
* * * * *

The Spectator

Member of I. I. P. A.

The Nation's Leading Prison Weekly —
7500 Copies Circulated Weekly

Heading
for the
GOLDE

40 NO. 39   4000 Cooper Street, Jackson, Michigan 49201   Friday, September 18, 1

Richard Herr (Center) served as Editor and artist
for the Prison newspaper "The Spectator"

Richard Herr enjoying a walk and cigar
in the Jackson Prison courtyard

Richard Herr competing on the Jackson Prison Tennis Courts

Richard Herr rushing the quarterback
during a Jackson Prison football game

Richard Herr with his arm around his tennis partner and fellow
convicted murderer Floyd "Butch" Tisi

Richard Herr posing with one of the many acts that entertained
prisoners at the Southern Michigan Prison

Richard Herr posing with a singer who came to
Jackson Prison to entertain the inmates

228

Richard Herr speaking with a university co-ed
who was visiting the Southern Michigan Prison

The Gymnils perform for the Southern Michigan Prison
inmates on April 8th, 1973. Richard Herr can be seen wearing
a vest standing in front of the stage

229

Richard Herr sitting on the lap of Bill Dominique,
with "Butch" Tisi on the lap of Morgan Clark

Richard Herr (smoking cigar) and friends watching a
football game in the Prison Newspaper offices

Richard Herr (left) relaxing in prison with other inmates,
spinning records and having a "drink"

Richard Herr and friends hanging out in **The Spectator** offices

Richard Herr and other inmates conferring
with a prison official

Richard Herr posing with leaders
of Jackson Prisons "Black Mafia"

Richard Herr (wearing glasses) in the prison cafeteria

Richard Herr riding a donkey and enjoying a cigar
on the Jackson Prison grounds

Pauline Herr (Far Right) speaking with her Husband Richard (kneeling on stage) after a performance at the prison theatre

Editor Richard Herr handing out copies of the prison newspaper **The Spectator** in the lobby area of Jackson Prison

Richard Herr (far left smoking a cigar with sunglasses) with members of Jackson Prison's "Black Mafia" including Chuck Ewing, Chuck Mathews, and James Clark (1968)

Paul "Harry" DeRose (Right) introducing Blackstone the Magician to then Lansing Mayor Ralph W. Crego

CHAPTER 16

THE MURDER OF BETTY REYNOLDS

*"Murder is not about lust and it's not about violence.
It's about possession. When you feel the last breath
of life coming out of the woman, you look into her eyes.
At that point, it's being God."*

Ted Bundy

Over my forty five plus years I have heard several theories about the Murder of Betty Reynolds. I think most bore a degree of semblance of what may have taken place, but none were ever the complete truth. I don't think I can ever for sure know the motive or reason for the brutal murder of the beautiful mother of two, Richard Herr is the only person who can answer that question and he obviously isn't telling. However, through a great deal of research and my knowledge of the perpetrator, I have a good idea of what happened on that beautiful summer day just outside of Grand Ledge.

The sun showed brightly in the clear summer sky on that early afternoon as the smell of freshly cut grass filled the air along Lawson road. Betty Reynolds had just finished mowing her well-manicured yard. The homes in this area were sparsely placed, separated by wooded hollows, fenced in fields, and clear pastures. The white shuttered red cottage sat across from a corn field and next to a field fenced with split rails. A giant willow tree shaded the driveway. The quaint home had a nice patio with a grill and swimming pool in back, and is on a rise with the Grand River down below. A small barn sat behind the home where the Reynolds kept a horse, two dogs, and a few ducks and chickens.

A blue Ford with white sidewalls pulls into the gravel driveway, of the home that sat just a few hundred yards in front of the winding Grand River, turning up a cloud of dust; it was 12:50 p.m. Jill and Penny Reynolds, ages 11 and 7, were playing in the living room when the strange car with the sharply dressed man arrived at their home. They had never seen him before. My father, wearing dark brown slacks, a light blue dress shirt, and a white sport coat with a thin plaid of yellow, dark green, brown, and black, walked from the car up to the small home where he rang the doorbell. He was greeted by the young girls and asked if he could speak to their mother. The petite blonde haired Betty Reynolds who was still dressed in the bikini she had been wearing while mowing the lawn a few minutes earlier came to the door from the kitchen and greeted the stranger. They made small talk and she giggled lightly as she let him in. She then led him to the kitchen and asked him to take a seat for a moment. Betty then quickly went into the bedroom and grabbed a white terry robe to cover herself. The two sat in the kitchen where my father and Mrs. Reynolds talked for several minutes. The girls remained in the living room.

The nature of the conversation between Betty and my father can only be known by the two of them. My father in his confession and in his book has consistently said that he drove to the Reynolds residence that day to address the problem with the title on the Oldsmobile the Reynolds had purchased from Crain's, but he was terminated from the lot that made the sale a few weeks prior and the transaction was six months earlier? My father was a philanderer, and some have speculated that he went to the Reynolds home that day because he knew the Reynolds were having problems with their marriage and there were rumors that Betty had once posed for nude photos. She was an attractive woman and some have even speculated that she and my father may have been seeing each-other; police were investigating a tip that my dad had visited Betty during her week stay at Lansing General Hospital in April of 1966 after her hysterectomy. Unfortunately the investigation into this theory was no longer pursued after my father pled guilty to the crime.

Whatever the conversation that early afternoon, Betty felt the need to send the children to the neighbors where the 14yr old girl who lived there, Shelly Bush, regularly babysat. Betty walked outside with Jill and Penny and went about twenty-five feet from the house when the visitor yelled out from the front door "Don't go any further." The girls were instructed not to return to the house until the man's car was gone. The girls heard the man warn their mother not to go any further as she led them out of the home, their mother was shaky and the stranger frightened the girls. The daughters told police that the visitor wouldn't allow their Mother to make a phone call. This report given by the children conflicts with the story my father tells in his book *Inside-Outside*, where he said that Mrs. Reynolds made several attempts to call her husband at work.

Once back inside, things must have gone very badly rather quickly. Betty did find a few seconds to scribble a small note that read "Police" and place it on the threshold of the sliding screen door that led to the back deck off the kitchen. We may never know the why, but what is known is that a struggle then ensued, from the trail of blood it is believed the attack most likely started in the kitchen and then into the master bedroom. My father's account in his book gives some insight, and then when we apply what we know from the police reports and from what the Coroner reported, as well as what we know about Betty Reynolds and Richard Herr, it is easier to deduce what may have happened on that sunny July afternoon.

From *Inside-Outside* by Richard Herr:

> "...I turned quickly and glimpsed something shiny in her hand. Without hesitation I swung around and struck out towards her thoroughly as I had been taught to do in Karate training. I hit her arm, sending her spinning around; without thinking I

slammed my right fist into the side of her head.
She dropped to the floor with a thud. She didn't
appear unconscious, but I knew she was seriously
injured. There was blood dripping from the point of
impact where my fist hit her temple."

The autopsy report stated that Mrs. Reynolds took an initial blow to the head near the temple with the kitchen butchers knife. The Coroner states that "considerable prolonged bleeding could have occurred from the stab wound to the left side of the head without interfering with muscular activity or consciousness".

It wasn't my father's fist that struck Betty Reynolds in the side of the head, but a seven inch serrated butcher's knife. This explains the considerable amount of blood in the bedroom. The bed itself was blood soaked. Mrs. Reynolds most assuredly had to have fallen to the floor from such a blow. My father states that he "glimpsed something shiny in her hand"; she may have grabbed the knife in fear of her safety. He was obviously able to disarm and turn the weapon back on the Grand Ledge house wife.

My father's account in his book has him laying Betty in the bed after his initial strike. The coroner's reports state that the victim was struck in a manner that still allowed her motor skills. At this time the thirty-seven year old mother was now nude. Her bottoms and robe left on the living room floor. Why? Was there a sexual advance made?

Betty Reynolds must have come to when on the bed, and seeing an opportunity, she sent her naked body through the bay window of her bedroom and onto her side lawn, cutting up her feet in the process and leaving shards of glass imbedded in each foot.   In absolute terror, she must have seen an opportunity and fled for her life. Betty tried to run to the safety of the woods, but the murderer followed her through the window and chased her into the wooded area towards the Grand River, jabbing the knife at her from behind. The coroner noted lacerations and bruising on the victims back and arms that indicate she was being slashed at by the dull blade as she fled.

As the naked victim ran into the wooded area down towards the Grand River, she got tangled up in a barbed wire fence along the shore just a few yards from the water, and this is where Betty Reynolds met her death. It is a very steep drop from the Reynolds property down to the river and it would be easy to assume that the victim lost her balance. With her feet tangled in the fence, a blade penetrated her back and pierced her heart and back bone through to her front. The murderer had the forethought to grab the tasseled tie from Betty's white robe as he left the house in pursuit, and used it to bind the victim's hands behind her back, hog tying her. The coroner's report suggests that Mrs. Reynolds was nearing death, but still living at this time.

The victim faced her assailant as she was bludgeoned. The murderer took the dull kitchen knife and started to slash the woman's throat. He slashed at it, over and over, trying to separate it from the bone until her head was nearly completely severed in what Pathologist Dr. Charles E. Black termed a "coup de grace type (of killing) to ensure certain death". Betty Reynolds was now dead, her five foot-three inch, one hundred and three pound nude frame had been left in the woods with over forty stab wounds and multiple lacerations, nearly decapitated, her hands tied behind her back grasping the bloodied ferns around her body, with branches still tightly clenched in her hands as her body fell lifeless.   It would be eight hours before a police tracking dog brought up from Jackson, Oede, located her lifeless twisted body just feet from the river.

My father returned to the Reynolds home, the authorities suspect "to wait for the children to return." Eaton County Sheriff Elwin Smith theorized that the killer returned to the house to wait for the children to return, and then kill the only witnesses. "He was within a few feet of the river and, if he wanted to dispose of the knife, he could have. He apparently wasn't done with it." He collected his clothing and washed as much blood off of him as possible. He was supposed to be at the Doctors office having his hand examined at this time, and couldn't wait at the home too long.

It is known that Betty's swimsuit bottoms and blood strained terry robe were left in the living area, and her blood soaked top was found in a bag of used bottles and cans on the steps leading down to the finished basement. The killer obviously tried to wash himself off in the basement sink, as watered down blood splattering covered the area, and leaving little thought to what he touched as several fingerprints of the assailant were taken from the scene by detectives. The main upstairs bathroom was in a similar condition, with monogrammed towels wiped with blood strewn about and watered down blood stains spotting the bathroom sink and tile walls. There were also shards of glass and particles of grass and weeds adhering to the edges of the sink.

The entirety of the crime took place in less than an hour and fifteen minute window, the daughters returned to the home at two fifteen that afternoon with their babysitter Shelly Bush, there simply was no time for anyone else to commit the crime.

242

My father fled the scene leaving the authorities with an abundance of evidence. The murderer jumped into his car and tried to start it, it stalled on him three times as he tells in his book, before he was finally able to regroup himself and drive from the carnage near the river. He claims in his account that he was disoriented, with a "buzzing noise" in his head as he fled the scene. He apparently had the sense to grab one of the monogrammed towels from the upstairs bathroom to continue to clean him-self up, it was found the next day caught on a wire fence near the corners of Waverly and Mount Hope roads, miles from the Reynolds home. This is the route my dad said in his book he drove after leaving Grand Ledge.

I have to believe that my father then went home at this time, where my mother and the baby were luckily out shopping. My mom would have certainly questioned my father about the blood on his clothing, and would not have relented until she received an answer she was satisfied with. If you consider what he had just done and his state of mind at that moment, and then add in the couple's turbulent history; it probably wouldn't have been a good outcome for my mother and sister had they been there when he arrived home.

At home alone, my father had the time to clean himself up, get rid of the clothing he had been wearing, and re-dress. The sports coat he wore to work, and then to the Reynolds that day was never found. My father then called Jack Dykstra Ford from the house on Holmes Street and spoke with his manager Jim Elder at around 3:00 p.m. and told him he was having trouble finding the company doctor's office. This frustrated my father's supervisor; he had been gone for nearly three hours and was just now calling for directions? The company doctor, William Meade, had his office on Michigan Ave., just three blocks from my parent's house. My father arrived at the doctor's office at 3:30 to see the company physician, but he was now unavailable so he instead saw the physician on hand, Dr. Omero Iung, who tended to the injury to my father's hand which was both lacerated and fractured. The fracture I am certain came from him slamming his hand in the car door at dealership earlier that day, but the laceration had to be from the struggle with Betty Reynolds and the glass from the window. He had cut his hand earlier, but it was bandaged when he arrived at the Reynolds' Home. The Reynolds children gave the Police an extremely detailed description of the suspect, and a large bandage on my father's hand would have been very noticeable. He had a small laceration on his finger that was covered by a flesh colored Band-Aid at the time he left the dealership and headed to Grand Ledge.

Imagine the desperation my father must have been experiencing in order to purposely slam his finger in the car door at the dealership knowing it would allow him to be able to leave his job and drive to the Reynolds home. What caused this type of severe behavior is only known by him.

After finishing up at the doctor's my father returned home where my mother had already returned with Dorette after shopping with her friend Dixie. My dad never admitted to being at the Reynolds home to my mother until just prior to his confessing of the crime in court. His stories on what happened this day have constantly changed. I do not think he will ever tell the complete truth. I have read that only a sociopath is able to commit a crime with the level of brutality that Betty Reynolds experienced and then be able to go about his daily life as if he had done nothing, showing no emotion or signs of distress. This is my father.

244

CHAPTER 17

SINS OF THE FATHER

"Yet you say, 'Why should not the son suffer for the iniquity of the Father?' When the son has done what is just and right, and has been careful to observe all my statutes, he shall surely live. The soul who sins shall die. The son shall not suffer for the iniquity of the father, nor the father for the iniquity of the son. The righteousness of the righteous shall be upon himself, and the wickedness of the wicked shall be upon himself.'

Ezekiel 18:19-20

They say that time heals all wounds, this may be so, but the scars still remain. Most of the people associated with my father's case are dead and gone. Others have moved away from the Lansing area to whereabouts unknown. All of the judges and attorneys, from both the prosecution and defense, and from every hearing, are deceased. Jack Reynolds and his daughters moved away from the Lansing area long ago. The old Reynolds home along Lawson road in Grand Ledge still stands much older and warn, weathered by the elements and time. The small red barn to the rear of the home now has a lean to it, and the swimming pool is still there in the side yard, weeds weaved into the fence surrounding it, looking as if it is seldom if ever used.

Viewing the steepness of the incline down to the Grand River where Betty Reynolds took her last breath, one immediately notes that the drop off is so severe it would be difficult for one to stand straight without falling. For those still alive that remember my father's trial and the murder, it may be a memory that is not top of mind, but one that had been long filed away. After all, it has been nearly fifty years. That was until my father published his book and aroused sleeping memories of the crime.

Clearing the reputations of my mother and my grandfather, as well as answering the accusations from my father's tale were the initial reasons for me looking into the history of his trial and the murder of Betty Reynolds. I wrote earlier that I wanted to set the record straight for my children, but in truth, this was done as much for me as anyone. There were just too many unanswered questions and too many stories that made no sense to me. I wanted to know the truth for myself and for my sisters as well.

There were times that I was afraid of what I might find. I asked my wife Stacy early on, what if I find out my dad is innocent? She told me to "...just let the facts take you where they do." In truth, I would have loved to have found that my father was innocent of the horrific murder he was convicted of. I would have relished in sharing my discovery with all of those who had made life so difficult for me when I was young. It would have been a vindication for not only my father, but for our entire family!

Unfortunately what I found after countless hours of research, scrolling through micro-phish, scouring through transcripts and police reports, reading through old newspaper and magazine accounts, and interviewing different witnesses, was that Richard George Herr Jr., and nobody else, murdered Betty Reynolds on that hot summer day in 1966. There cannot be any doubt.

When arrested, and in earlier stories, Richard Herr had always claimed that he was not at the Reynolds home that day, he claimed he was at the doctor's office. He told Detective Keith before he was charged with the murder that he had not been in Grand Ledge. This is again the claim my father made during his appeal in 1973, where he states that he had not been at the Reynolds home in Grand Ledge that day and that his attorney had made up his confession for him. However, in his book *Inside Outside*, my father admits in his first pages to being in the Reynolds home the day of the murder and striking the victim Betty Reynolds. When someone lies so many different times it becomes harder and harder for them to remember what they told who and the story starts to change. That is the case with my father's story; it is a constantly changing tale. I am certain that when he wrote his book he was relying on the fact that in Michigan old court records and evidence

247

are destroyed after twenty five years. And that is still the case. However his case, because it was a murder case and such a brutal one at that, all of the records were saved and preserved by the authorities.

My father has a real knack for rearranging events and facts to confuse those who may have a memory of the murder that occurred outside the quiet village of Grand Ledge nearly fifty years ago. He states in his book that he slammed his finger in the car door AFTER leaving the Reynolds home. This is important because the whole basis of my father's defense was that he was at the doctor's office having his finger looked at during the time of the murder, so he couldn't have possibly been anywhere near Grand Ledge. In all my father's defense testimonies he states that he slammed his finger in a car door at the car dealership and was then sent to see the company doctor on Michigan Ave. This fact is also confirmed in a police report where detectives interview the then floor manager of Jack Dykstra Ford, Jim Elder. As I said, it is difficult for a liar to keep track of all of his lies, especially over forty-five plus years.

My father's palm print on the butcher's knife, the murder weapon, cannot be explained away. There is no way that in 1966 someone could have placed his palm-print, made in the victim's blood, on the murder weapon and have it appear so clearly. This becomes even harder to accept when you learn that the print was made three days prior to him being arrested...although that is what he is asking the readers of his book to believe.

Richard Herr never asked for a lie detector test. It wasn't until after he had pled guilty that his claim that he was denied a polygraph emerged. When he was initially arrested on Monday July 11th, 1966, he refused one. When you read my father's book, one would think that he was kept from taking a polygraph test. There was no need for the authorities to give him a lie detector test after he confessed to the murder, they had their man. Although inadmissible, my father could have requested, and even insisted, that his defense attorneys arrange for him to take an independent polygraph exam. It never happened. During his appeal in 1973 his former defense attorney Leo Farhat testified that his client had never requested a polygraph exam. The reality is that my father could submit himself to a polygraph test today if he really wanted to try and exonerate himself. It was safer for him to write his book of lies instead. He could control the outcome.

My father also strongly insinuates in his book that his defense attorney, Leo Farhat, forced him to plead guilty. If this was the case, he had an opportunity to change attorneys prior to his plea, and also an opportunity to tell Judge Robinson in chambers, where it was just him and the Judge, that he was being forced to confess against his will. He did neither. In fact Judge Robinson asked him while accepting the guilty plea if he had been threatened or forced to make a plea. The answer was "no." My father accepted the plea bargain because he knew he was guilty and he didn't want to spend the rest of his life behind bars.

I am certain that Farhat strongly suggested that accepting the plea for second degree murder was my father's best option, but that is much different than forcing someone. And in hindsight, it turned out to be his best option. He served twelve years in prison for a murder that, had it been committed in Florida or Texas at that time, would have seen him receive the death penalty. He should be eternally grateful for what Leo Farhat did for him. My father accepting the plea to murder has also allowed him to make his ongoing claims that he was denied a trial and has allowed him to lie about his case.

My father has never been grateful for the loyalty he received from my mother. Her eight years of vigilant support from the time of his arrest through his appeal, up until the time they divorced. Her devotion to her husband, despite the hardships and shame it brought her has never been fully appreciated by my dad. She had become somewhat of a pariah in the community due to her unwavering support for Richard Herr. He expected this type of loyalty, and took it for granted. He also took advantage of it at the expense of his children. Him having expensive cigars, magazine subscriptions, and specific clothing took priority over his children being properly clothed, fed, and cared for.

Richard Herr also never appreciated the support he received from his in-laws, particularly his father-in-law Paul "Harry" DeRose. My grandfather spent thousands upon thousands of dollars to assist my dad with his defense. In my father's book, he praises the two attorneys my grandfather hired to help him; first Joe Louisell, then later Ted Albert. Without my grandfather, there would have been no Joe Louisell, and later on, no appeal with Ted Albert. He never so much as thanked his father-in-law for his help, even at a time when his own parents had abandoned him and left the state during his appeal. He instead chose to defame my grandfather with malicious lies and insinuations in his book. He did so years after my grandfather had passed.

My dad has also never shown any remorse or contrition for his crime, or for the victims. I often wonder what happened to the Reynolds children, Jill and Penny. What kind of life did they end up living because of my father's terrible deed? What became of John "Jack" Reynolds? Was he able to ever move on from this painful moment of his life?   The pain and terror my father inflicted on Betty Reynolds that July afternoon has never truly been answered for. Twelve years for such a deed is not justice.

My father has also never had any consideration for how his crime has affected his own family. How it affected his children. His actions over these forty plus years suggest he simply never cared. It was always about him; about his needs, his desires, and his wants.   I know how his murder of Betty Reynolds affected me, my mother and my sisters. My mother has never really recovered from the pain and shame the crime brought her. To this day she secludes herself in her home every year from July 7th through July 11th. I don't know if she is re-living that time or mourning what she feels she lost on those dates back in 1966. I do know that as a kid growing up I never understood it and was always a bit scared during those early July days as my mother would not let us go outside between these dates. We were confined to our home, not allowed to go out and play with friends, unable to enjoy these mid-summer days during our youth. We were told nothing good happens between these days and it is better to stay home.   She is still best of friends with Dixie, the woman she went shopping with on the day of the murder. They speak and visit several times a week.

My sisters and I have moved on the best that we could. We have all had our own issues and difficulties brought on from our heritage and upbringing, but we have all succeeded in overcoming many of the obstacles we faced.

In my adult life, I had given very little thought to my father and his crime. I was too busy with my own life and the challenges that every day brings.   In fact, I have gone years without a thought of him. I had never developed a bond with my father, he was never around. My dad had only been a negative influence on my life, so why have a relationship? When I turned eighteen, one of the first things I did was change my name to DeRose in honor of my grandfather. My sisters felt differently, as each of them would speak and visit with my father from time to time. Even then, their contact was sparse unless he needed something.

Richard Herr has been able to rebuild his life after serving only twelve years of his 25-40 year sentence. Today he lives with his wife Michelle in Flagstaff Arizona where he has been able to re-establish himself and create a new life. He started a new family, having two additional daughters, Jessica and Katherine, who are today both adults. This never bothered me, I was just happy that he was not around me, and no longer living in the area. America is the home of second chances, and according to the State of Michigan my father had paid his debt to society. Now he was living his new life, and I was fine with that. As British author Graham Greene once said, "A murderer is regarded by the conventional world as something almost monstrous, but a murderer to himself is only an ordinary man." My father now portrays himself as an ordinary man.

Just as my father has been granted a second chance by society, my sisters and I should never again be judged by the sins of my father. The conflicts I encountered as the murderers son, the taunting and bullying I experienced along with the shame of my father's crime, although painful, forged me into the person I am today. It made me determined and strong willed. It forced me

252

to walk the straight and narrow as a teen, as I knew I was always going to be watched and judged by my father's history. I had two choices; I could let his history define me, or I could draw strength from my own experiences and use the lessons that I had learned to define myself. I became determined to create my own reputation and to be judged by my own actions. I may be the murderer's son, but he was not me. In truth, today he is a stranger to me.

Some who read this may equate my story with that of a Greek tragedy, a son attacking his father on behalf of his mother, almost Oedipal. I say that it is an American tragedy. The full title of my father's book is *Inside-Outside: to be continued*, however there is no longer any reason for him to continue his story, I have continued it for him. The real tragedy is that my father was able to publish his tale of lies, undeterred by the Son of Sam Law which should have prevented his book from being published in the first place.

The history of Richard Herr's case and the Murder of Betty Reynolds is now here in these pages for the world to see. There can be no more lies or half-truths, for all of the facts in these pages regarding the murder of Betty Reynolds, the investigation, and the trial, are supported by real and true evidence.

Every family has secrets that they hide, skeletons in the closet they pretend don't exist. There are the relatives they wish not to acknowledge. My father's book forced me to face all of these. The scab that was peeled back by my father's book is now healing, the wound once again fading, soon to be gone forever.

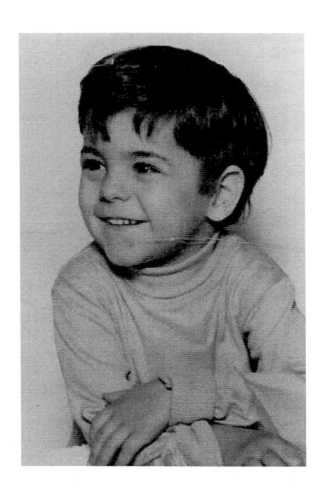

"A lot of life is dealing with your curse, dealing with the cards you were given that aren't so nice. Does it make you into a monster, or can you temper it in some way, or accept it and go in some other direction?"

Wes Craven

Made in the USA
Monee, IL
23 April 2020

26624740R00152